ICELAND TRAVEL GUIDE 2024

VISIT SMART WITH INSIDER KNOWLEDGE ON THE FINEST ROUTES, MUST-SEES, AND SEASONAL ACTIVITIES

VERA STORME

VERA STORME

CONTENTS

1 INTRODUCTION

T hank you so much for choosing this book to visit Iceland! I truly appreciate it, and I've done my best to make it as helpful as possible. This guide will give you all the basic information you need, and i designed it to help you get the most out of the trip.

Think of it as having a friend by your side, sharing tips and advice along the way.

The first time I set foot here, I remember this overwhelming sense of space, the kind that almost humbles you. It wasn't just the vast, sweeping landscapes that hit me, but the feeling that **I'd entered a place where the earth itself was alive.** You don't just see Iceland's beauty; you feel it. There's an unspoken power in the air, a quiet reminder that nature is still in charge here. **I still recall my first drive from the airport to Reykjavik**—the landscape was like nothing I'd ever seen before. The mountains rose sharply from the earth, the sky stretched endlessly above, and the land seemed to whisper stories of old. Right then, I knew this wouldn't be just another trip. It felt more like stepping into an epic saga, where every turn of the road reveals a new chapter.

Why should you visit Iceland? Simply put, it's unlike anywhere else you've ever been. And I know people throw that phrase around a lot, but here, it actually rings true. There's something in the way the untouched, raw beauty of the place just takes over your senses. You've got towering glaciers, volcanic landscapes that feel like they belong on another planet, and geothermal hot springs that steam away in the middle of stark, almost alien terrain. **It's a place where adventure and serenity meet**—you might hike across a glacier one morning and soak in a natural hot spring by afternoon. You come here for the big, breathtaking moments that take you out of your everyday life and remind you just how incredible this planet is.

Now, geographically speaking, Iceland is in a league of its own. **It sits right on the edge of the Arctic Circle**, caught between North America and Europe, but it feels like its own world entirely. **There's this unique energy here**, literally, with all the volcanic activity happening beneath the surface. Iceland is still growing, still shifting, and you can feel that dynamism in the air. The geothermal power is so real, you can actually take a dip in a naturally heated pool in the middle of nowhere. **But be prepared for some extreme contrasts**, especially if you're visiting in winter or summer. In summer, you get this surreal midnight sun where it never really gets dark, and you'll have hours upon hours to explore. But in winter, the days are short, the darkness long—but that's when **the Northern Lights** come out to play, painting the sky in shades of green and purple that will make you forget the cold entirely.

The landscapes here are as diverse as they are dramatic. One minute you're walking on black sand beaches, with these towering basalt columns rising out of the sea like sentinels. The next, you're standing at the edge of a glacier, the ice crunching beneath your boots, with nothing but endless blue and white stretching before you. I remember standing at the base of Skógafoss, this massive waterfall, the spray misting my face, and it felt like the kind of place you see in fantasy films—unreal, yet absolutely real at the same time. **This country doesn't do ordinary.**

The people you meet here are another story altogether. **Icelanders have this wonderful warmth**, and they're fiercely proud of their land and culture. They've got this laid-back vibe that's contagious, but there's also a deep connection to their Viking roots. **You'll notice it in the way they tell stories, especially about the sagas and folklore**. Don't be surprised if someone casually mentions the "huldufólk"— hidden people—like it's the most natural thing in the world. Icelanders don't just live on this land; they live with it, in a way that's rare to see. They respect it deeply, and as a visitor, you're expected to do the same.

The history here is rich, too. Iceland was settled by Norse explorers in the 9th century, and that Viking spirit still lingers. It's a nation that fought for its independence—literally, during times of hardship—and it shows. **The island might feel remote, but it's never isolated in spirit.** You'll find modern Reykjavik buzzing with creativity, innovation, and sustainability. They've embraced the future while holding onto the past, and that balance is what makes it feel so different from anywhere else.

One of the things that truly sets Iceland apart is **how they've harnessed the power of the earth to create one of the most sustainable countries on the planet.** Almost all of their energy comes from renewable sources, mainly geothermal and hydropower. And they're passionate about preserving the environment. You'll notice it as you travel around—**Icelanders live lightly on the land**, and as a visitor, you're encouraged to do the same. **It's not just a vacation spot; it's a place that asks you to slow down, look around, and really think about your connection to the natural world.**

So, when should you visit? Well, that depends on what kind of experience you're after. **Summer is perfect if you're into hiking, long road trips, and soaking up the midnight sun.** You'll have nearly 24 hours of daylight, which is wild at first, but you'll quickly appreciate how much you can pack into a day. **Winter, though, is pure magic—** the Northern Lights dancing in the sky, snow-covered landscapes, and the cozy warmth of Icelandic hospitality to welcome you after a day of exploring. Just be prepared for shorter days and unpredictable weather, but honestly, that just adds to the adventure. **Spring and autumn offer a quieter charm**, with fewer tourists, cooler temperatures, and the landscape either coming alive with blooms or painting itself in shades of red and gold.

So what should you expect when you arrive? For one, safety—this is one of the safest countries you'll ever visit, and you'll feel that peace of mind from the moment you land. People here speak English fluently, so communication is easy, and the infrastructure is top-notch. **But what will stand out the most is the feeling that you've stepped into a place that's both ancient and modern, familiar yet completely foreign.** It's a country that invites you to explore its mysteries, to dive deep into its landscapes, and to walk away with experiences that are anything but ordinary.

Now, what about money? Let's talk local currency. Iceland uses the Icelandic króna (ISK). It might feel unfamiliar at first, but it's simple once you get the hang of it. **Most places in Iceland accept credit or debit cards**, and they're used far more frequently than cash. In fact, in some of the smaller towns, cash might even be a bit of a rarity. But, if you want to feel prepared, here's a quick guide on how to handle money during your trip.

When you arrive, **you'll notice that the currency exchange counters at Keflavík Airport or ATMs** offer an easy way to get some ISK if you prefer to have cash on hand. You can also withdraw cash from ATMs, which are widely available in most towns and cities. However, if you're planning on sticking mostly to Reykjavik or popular tourist spots, you might not need to worry about cash at all. I personally found that I used my card for everything—from paying for meals to booking tours or buying souvenirs.

So, how does the currency break down? The Icelandic króna (ISK) comes in denominations of 1,000, 5,000, and 10,000 ISK notes, as well as coins in values of 1, 5, 10, 50, and 100 ISK. Don't be shocked by the high numbers—1,000 ISK is roughly equivalent to about 7 or 8 euros or 8 to 9 U.S. dollars, depending on the exchange rate. It can seem a bit strange at first when you're looking at a menu and see something priced at 2,500 ISK for a meal, but once you convert it, it makes more sense.

2 THE CAPITAL

2.1 REYKJAVIK

n **Reykjavik**, you'll notice how compact the city is, which makes exploring incredibly easy. You can walk from the **Old Harbor** to **Hallgrímskirkja**, the tallest church, in about 15 minutes, and in between, you'll pass colorful houses, small parks, and plenty of cafés. The streets are clean, and you'll always feel close to nature because you can see the mountains on one side and the ocean on the other as you move through the city. There are no skyscrapers, and that keeps everything feeling open, with nothing blocking the sky, which changes color constantly with the light and weather.

Hallgrímskirkja is the best way to see the whole city in one glance. You'll want to go up to the top for the view because it shows you just how small and easy to navigate the city really is. The church itself is built in a unique style that reflects Iceland's volcanic basalt columns, so it's not just a viewpoint but an important architectural landmark. Right nearby is **Harpa Concert Hall**, a modern building made entirely of glass panels that shimmer with the changing light of the sky.

Harpa's glass reflects both the ocean and the sky, making it a spot that's worth walking around even if you're not attending a concert. It's a key part of Reykjavik's creative energy, home to music festivals, performances, and events that pull in visitors from all over the world.

You'll want to walk down to the **Old Harbor**. It's still used by local fishermen, and you can see the small boats lined up early in the morning, which makes it feel like a working part of the city even with all the tourists visiting for whale-watching tours. The area has been updated in the last few years with new seafood restaurants and shops, but it still holds onto that old-world feel, with weathered buildings and a sense that the sea has always been central to life here. The seafood is incredibly fresh—you can sit down for a meal of **lamb stew** or **plokkfiskur** at one of the restaurants nearby, or even try some fresh-caught fish straight from the harbor.

Everything in the city is **geothermally powered**, which means the hot water you use comes straight from natural sources. This makes the whole city eco-friendly, and you'll notice that many of the buses are electric, and almost all homes and businesses run on sustainable energy. There's no need to worry about pollution here because Reykjavik prides itself on keeping things clean and green, which is part of why the air feels so fresh.

Art is everywhere in Reykjavik. As you walk through the streets, you'll come across **murals** and **street art** on the sides of buildings that tell stories of Iceland's history and its connection to nature. These are commissioned works, so they're not just random graffiti—they're part of the city's cultural identity, changing over time as new works are added. You'll find that the city is a center for creativity, with **art galleries** that highlight Icelandic artists and a vibrant scene that blends old and new, traditional and modern.

Most people here speak English fluently, so you won't have any trouble getting around or asking for directions. Reykjavik is also one of the safest cities you'll ever visit. You can walk late at night through the main streets, and it feels completely secure, with people out enjoying the night at bars and cafés that stay open late, especially on weekends. Locals are friendly, and they love to share stories about the city or recommend their favorite places to eat or visit.

Everything in Reykjavik is close. You can take a bus, but walking or biking is even better because you'll see so much more. If you're looking for places to eat, there's a good mix of traditional Icelandic food like **fermented shark** and **lamb**, alongside modern cuisine that mixes local ingredients with global influences. The city isn't cheap, so meals can be pricey, but it's worth trying at least one good seafood meal while you're here because the fish is as fresh as it gets.

2.2 TRANSPORTATION IN REYKJAVIK

You'll find that **walking** is the most practical way to visit the center of the city. Since the main attractions like **Harpa**, **Hallgrímskirkja**, and the **Old Harbor** are so close to each other, you won't need to rely on transportation for most of your time in the city center. The streets are laid out in a way that makes it easy to navigate, and there are plenty of signs to guide you. For example, from **Laugavegur** (the main shopping street), you can reach **Hallgrímskirkja** in just about 10 minutes by foot, and from there, it's another 5 minutes to the **Old Harbor**. There's no need to rush, and walking will let you take in the little things, like street art and local shops, along the way.

When walking isn't enough, the **Strætó bus system** is reliable and easy to use. The buses run frequently during the day, starting around **6:30 AM** on weekdays and around **9 AM** on weekends. During peak hours, buses run every **15-30 minutes**, depending on the route. You'll want to download the **Strætó app** because that's how you'll pay for your ticket. It costs about **490 ISK** for a one-way trip, which is roughly **$3.50**, and your ticket is valid for **75 minutes**, meaning you can switch buses without paying again during that time. The app shows live bus schedules and stops, making it easy to plan your trip in real-time. There are plenty of bus stops in the city center, with major stops near **Lækjartorg**, **Hlemmur**, and **BSÍ bus terminal**. If you're planning to take multiple trips, you can also buy a **day pass** for about **1,800 ISK** ($12), which gives you unlimited travel for 24 hours. Just be aware that after **11 PM**, the buses run less frequently, so if you're staying out late, check the schedule in advance.

For something faster, **taxis** are available, but they're more expensive compared to buses. You can use the **Hreyfill app** to order a taxi, and they usually arrive within minutes if you're in the city center. Most taxis start at **1,000 ISK** (around **$7**), and the fare goes up based on distance, so a short trip within the center might cost you about **2,000 ISK** ($14) or more. It's a good option if you're carrying luggage or don't want to wait for a bus, but for longer rides, it can get pricey quickly. You'll find taxis waiting at popular spots like **Harpa** or the **BSÍ bus terminal**, but using the app ensures a ride is never too far away. They run 24/7, so even if you're out late, you won't be stranded, but it's smart to factor in the cost, especially for trips to or from the airport, where a taxi can run upwards of **16,000 ISK** ($110).

If you prefer more flexibility, **biking** is a great way to get around, especially if you want to explore areas a bit further from the city center. You can rent bikes from places like **Reykjavik Bike Tours** or **Bike Company**, both located near the **Old Harbor**. A typical bike rental costs about **3,000 ISK** ($21) per day, and many rental shops also offer multi-day deals if you plan on staying longer. Reykjavik's bike lanes are well-marked, and the city's mostly flat terrain makes biking easy for everyone. For example, if you want to ride to **Elliðaárdalur**, a scenic park on the outskirts, it's a quick 20-minute ride from downtown. The bike paths are clear, and you'll pass by green spaces, rivers, and even small waterfalls. Biking is especially fun in the summer, when the daylight lasts well into the evening.

For a quicker, easy-to-use option, there are **electric scooters** all over the city. These scooters, run by **Hopp**, are perfect for short trips. They're easy to spot, and you'll find them parked around the city center. To use one, download the **Hopp app**, find a nearby scooter, and unlock it by scanning the QR code. The price starts at around **50 ISK** ($0.35) per minute, and you can leave the scooter almost anywhere when you're done. Scooters are ideal for zipping between spots that are too far to walk but not worth the wait for a bus or taxi. For example, if you want to ride from **Harpa** to the **National Museum**, it takes about 5 minutes on a scooter, and the ride will cost you less than **500 ISK** ($3.50). Scooters are available throughout the day and night, though they're most convenient for quick, daytime trips around the city.

2.3 TOP ATTRACTIONS

You'll find **Hallgrímskirkja** right at the top of **Skólavörðustígur**, and from anywhere in the city, its tall, striking shape stands out, making it impossible to miss. This is the tallest building around, and you can take the elevator straight to the top for the best views in the city. From up there, you can see everything—the colorful rooftops, the surrounding mountains, and the sea that wraps around the city. It's not free to go up; the tower entrance fee is **1,200 ISK**, which is around **$8.50**, but the experience is well worth it because the view gives you a real sense of how the city is laid out, and it's open from **9 AM to 9 PM** during the summer months, though in winter it closes earlier at **5 PM**. Inside the church, you can't miss the massive pipe organ, and the sheer size of it—**5,275 pipes**—fills the whole space with its presence, even when it's silent.

Next, you can head down to **Harpa Concert Hall**, which is located right on **Austurbakki** by the water, not far from the main center. Harpa is hard to miss because its entire structure is made of glass that changes color depending on the light, and when you walk inside, the first thing you'll notice is how the light reflects off the water and fills the huge open spaces. You don't need a ticket to enter Harpa itself, so you can walk around freely, enjoying the views from inside the building. It's open from **8 AM to midnight**, so you can stop by any time. The glass panels make the whole building glow, and it's especially stunning when the sun is setting, casting pinks and oranges across the harbor. If you're interested in catching a concert or an event, tickets are available online, but you don't have to attend a show to enjoy the architecture and the atmosphere here.

Once you're ready to see the sea up close, the **Old Harbor** is just down **Geirsgata**. The harbor is always busy, with fishing boats and tour boats coming and going, and it's completely free to walk along the docks and enjoy the sights. The air smells like saltwater, and you can hear the seagulls as you watch the boats head out into the bay. If you're curious about marine life, the **Whales of Iceland** museum is nearby, but just walking along the harbor is an experience in itself. The best time to visit the harbor is during the day when the boat tours are in full swing, and the activity is lively, but you can come anytime since the area is open around the clock, though most tours and exhibitions tend to run during daylight hours.

2.4 A ONE-DAY ITINERARY IN REYKJAVIK

You start the day at **9 AM** by going straight to **Hallgrímskirkja**, right at the top of **Skólavörðustígur**, where you'll take the elevator to the top for **1,200 ISK** and get the best view of the city, seeing everything from the sea to the mountains in just one sweep. You'll need around **30 to 40 minutes** here, not just to take in the view but also to have a proper look at the impressive church interior, especially the massive pipe organ. Once you've soaked in the view, it's only a **10-minute walk** down **Skólavörðustígur** to **Harpa Concert Hall** on **Austurbakki**. No ticket is required to walk in, and the place is open from **8 AM to midnight**, so you'll have plenty of time to explore the glass structure with its constantly shifting reflections. You'll spend around **30 minutes** wandering through the open spaces, taking in the harbor views through those huge windows, and admiring the light play off the water.

When you're done, head towards the **Old Harbor**, just a quick **5-minute walk** along **Geirsgata**. This place is alive with boats constantly coming and going—whale-watching tours, fishing boats, you name it—and it's completely free to explore. The sea air is fresh, and you'll want to spend about **30 to 40 minutes** walking along the docks, watching the activity, or just enjoying the calmness that comes with being by the water. By around **12 PM**, you'll walk along **Sæbraut** to get to the **Sun Voyager** sculpture, which is about a **10-minute walk** from the harbor. It's a famous steel sculpture shaped like a Viking ship, and the backdrop of **Mount Esja** across the bay makes it an ideal spot for photos. You only need **15 minutes** or so here before moving on.

From the **Sun Voyager**, head towards the **National Museum of Iceland** on **Suðurgata**, which will take you about **20 minutes** on foot. The museum is open from **10 AM to 5 PM**, and once inside, you'll spend about **1 hour** exploring its exhibits that cover everything from Iceland's early settlement days to modern history. After you've taken in the museum's highlights, walk about **10 minutes** to **Tjörnin**, the city's central lake, where you'll enjoy a quiet **20-minute** walk around its edge. This is where locals come to relax, and the scene of the city reflected in the still water is something you won't want to miss.

By around **3 PM**, take a **10-minute taxi** ride up to **Perlan** on **Öskjuhlíð Hill**. Inside, you'll find interactive exhibits, including the must-see **ice cave**, and from the observation deck, you'll get another unbeatable view of the city and the surrounding landscapes. You'll spend around **1 hour** here, and the ticket price is **4,900 ISK**, making it a great way to end the day with both an indoor exhibition and an outdoor view that ties everything together. Afterward, you can head back to the city center to relax, having seen all the essential sights in one efficient day.

2.5 DINING

At **Messinn** on **Lækjargata 6B**, you're going to want to sit down and order the **plokkfiskur**. It's the traditional Icelandic fish stew, served right in a hot pan, rich and creamy with cod and potatoes, and you'll get that dark rye bread on the side, which is perfect for soaking up the sauce. The price is around **3,500 to 4,500 ISK**, and you're right in the center of town, so it's an easy stop, especially if you're exploring nearby.

For something fast and local, you'll head to **Bæjarins Beztu Pylsur** at **Tryggvagata 1**, where you can grab a hot dog that's a mix of lamb, pork, and beef, topped with crispy onions, sweet mustard, and remoulade. It's not just a quick snack—it's a must-try. Each hot dog is only about **600 ISK**, and it's located right near the **Old Harbor**, so if you're already wandering that area, it's an easy stop that's full of flavor in just a few bites.

For fine dining, **Dill** on **Hverfisgata 12** is where you'll find something completely different. It's Reykjavik's Michelin-starred gem, and you'll be served a tasting menu that highlights local ingredients in ways you've never experienced. You can expect dishes like **arctic char** or **foraged herbs**, and the menu is seasonal, meaning it changes with what's fresh. The tasting menu is priced at **19,900 ISK**, so it's a splurge, but if you want the best culinary experience the city has to offer, this is where you go.

If you're looking for a laid-back experience after visiting **Hallgrím-skirkja**, walk across the street to **Café Loki** on **Lokastígur 28**. You'll want to try their **lamb soup**, a hearty, warming dish that's perfect for the weather, or go for the **rye bread ice cream** if you're in the mood for something sweet. Prices here are between **2,000 and 3,500 ISK**, making it an affordable and cozy spot after a morning of sightseeing.

For fresh seafood with a modern twist, go to **Fiskfélagið (Fish Company)** at **Vesturgata 2a** near the **Old Harbor**. This is where you'll find dishes like **grilled cod** and **langoustine**, with a bit of a creative flair. Prices range from **5,000 to 7,000 ISK**, and it's perfect if you're looking for something a little more special, especially after spending the day by the harbor.

At **Snaps Bistro** on **Þórsgata 1**, close to **Hlemmur Square**, you can enjoy French-inspired dishes with a local twist. You'll find **moules frites** or the daily fish special, and it's a cozy place where locals and tourists mingle. Meals cost between **3,500 to 5,000 ISK**, and since it's just steps away from **Laugavegur**, it's a great stop after a day of shopping.

For a true taste, you have to go to **Matur og Drykkur** on **Granda-garður 2**, near the **Saga Museum**. This is where you'll try dishes like **cured lamb** or **smoked arctic char**, and if you're feeling bold, the **cod head** is something to experience. It's not just about eating—it's about tasting the history and culture of the island, with prices ranging from **4,000 to 6,000 ISK**. It's an easy stop if you're exploring the harbor area.

2.6 NIGHTLIFE

At **Kaffibarinn**, you're stepping into a place that comes alive as the night goes on. Located on **Bergstaðastræti 1**, this bar is known for its lively atmosphere, especially on weekends when DJs start playing and the crowd picks up. You'll be there from around **11 PM** when things start to heat up, and you won't leave until the early hours of the morning. The place stays open until **1 AM** on weekdays and pushes it until **4:30 AM** on weekends. Grab a beer for about **1,500 ISK**, or if you're in the mood for something stronger, cocktails go for **2,000 ISK**. Since it's right in the center of the action, walking from **Laugavegur** is a breeze, making it an easy spot to start your night or even finish it if you want to stay in one place.

When you want to catch some live music, you should go straight to **Húrra**, which you'll find on **Tryggvagata 22**. The venue has that underground vibe that makes it feel like a hidden gem in the city. Live performances range from indie rock bands to electronic sets, and depending on the night, you might stumble onto a real discovery. The crowd shows up for the music, not just for a night out, so you'll get a real sense of the local scene. It's open until **1 AM** on weekdays and **4:30 AM** on weekends, with entrance fees usually between **1,000 and 2,000 ISK**. The location is close to the harbor, and after spending the day by the water, it's the perfect place to dive into the city's music scene without going far.

For something more intimate, **Mengi** on **Óðinsgata 2** gives you a completely different experience. It's small and run by artists, which means the performances are more experimental, often mixing art, music, and theater into something that feels personal and creative. You'll need to check the schedule ahead, as events are varied, but tickets typically cost **2,500 to 3,500 ISK**. The venue is quiet and introspective, making it a great contrast to the louder nightlife spots.

Located just a **5-minute walk** from **Hallgrímskirkja**, it's easy to get there if you've been exploring the city center.

For a laid-back beer, **Kaldi Bar** on **Laugavegur 20b** is where you want to be. The bar is known for its craft beers, especially their signature **Kaldi** brew, and it's got that warm, welcoming atmosphere that makes it a perfect place to sit down and unwind. You're looking at **1,200 to 1,500 ISK** for a beer, and it's open until **1 AM** on weekdays and **3 AM** on weekends. Being on **Laugavegur**, it's right in the middle of everything, making it an easy stop if you're just walking through the city's main street.

For some culture experience, head to **Iðnó** on **Vonarstræti 3**, located right next to **Tjörnin**, the city's central lake. This is one of the oldest venues in the city, hosting a variety of events from theater performances to live music. It's a stunning building, and attending a show here feels like stepping into Reykjavik's cultural history. Tickets for events typically range between **2,500 and 5,000 ISK**, depending on the show. Since it's only a **10-minute walk** from **Lækjargata**, you'll easily find your way there after a day of wandering the city center.

For bigger events, **Harpa Concert Hall** on **Austurbakki** is where you'll catch some of the most significant performances in town, whether it's classical music, international artists, or large-scale productions. The acoustics in Harpa are world-class, and the building itself is a sight to see, especially when it lights up at night. Ticket prices range from **4,000 ISK** for smaller events to over **10,000 ISK** for more prominent shows. Harpa is open all day, from **8 AM to midnight**, and even if you don't catch a performance, walking through the building is an experience in itself.

If you want to dance, **Paloma** on **Naustin 1-3** is the place to go. The music is electronic, with house and techno taking over the basement, where the real energy is. The crowd stays until **4:30 AM** on weekends, and you'll need to pay a cover charge of about **1,500 to 2,000 ISK** depending on the DJ. You're looking at **1,500 ISK** for a beer, and being centrally located, it's a great spot after hopping around other places on **Laugavegur**.

For something completely different, try **Gaukurinn** on **Tryggva-gata 22**. This is the spot for alternative nightlife, with drag shows, comedy nights, and live music that leans towards rock and metal. It's an inclusive space, and the crowd is always welcoming, making it stand out from other venues in the city. Most nights, there's no cover charge unless there's a special event, and drinks are affordable, with beers starting at **1,200 ISK**. It's open until **1 AM** on weekdays and **3 AM** on weekends, and since it's right next to **Húrra**, you can easily go between the two if you're looking for a change in atmosphere.

2.7 SHOPPING

When you're walking down **Laugavegur**, Reykjavik's main shopping street, you'll notice it's filled with shops offering everything from local crafts to high-end design. Start by heading into **The Handknitting Association of Iceland** at **Skólavörðustígur 19**, just off Laugavegur. This place is where you'll find the famous **lopapeysa** sweaters, each one hand-knitted by local women. These wool sweaters are an essential part of Iceland's culture, and prices start around **18,000 ISK**. You'll also find scarves, hats, and mittens, all made from the same soft, durable Icelandic wool that's perfect for the cold.

If modern Icelandic design is more your style, make your way to **Farmers Market** in the Grandi district at **Hólmaslóð 2**. It's a bit of a walk from the city center but worth it if you're looking for something that combines traditional Icelandic materials like wool and leather with sleek, contemporary designs. Sweaters here start at **25,000 ISK**, and coats can go up to **50,000 ISK** or more, but the quality is exceptional, and these pieces are designed to last. The clean, minimalist aesthetic reflects Icelandic nature, so if you're into functional fashion with a modern twist, this is the spot.

On weekends, head to **Kolaportið**, the flea market near the Old Harbor at **Tryggvagata 19**. Open from **11 AM to 5 PM** on Saturdays and Sundays, this market is packed with everything from vintage clothes to handmade jewelry. You'll find some real treasures here, and the prices can be lower than in regular shops, especially if you're looking for unique finds. You can also try traditional Icelandic foods like **hákarl** (fermented shark) and dried fish while you browse. It's a different kind of shopping experience, more casual but full of surprises.

For more high-end local design, stop by **Kraum** at **Aðalstræti 10**, one of Reykjavik's oldest houses. This shop showcases work from Icelandic designers, including homeware, ceramics, and jewelry. Every piece has a modern edge but stays rooted in Icelandic tradition. You'll find smaller items like handcrafted jewelry starting at **5,000 ISK**, but there are also larger pieces like furniture if you're looking for something truly special to take home.

Another great spot for wool products is **Icewear**, located at **Bankastræti 2**, right in the middle of the shopping district. This store specializes in high-quality **lopapeysa** sweaters, blankets, and accessories like gloves and scarves. Sweaters here are priced around **20,000 ISK**, and the smaller items like wool socks or hats start at about **4,000 ISK**. If you're looking for functional clothing that also makes a great souvenir, this is where you'll find it.

For something unique and a bit more personal, visit **Aurora Reykjavik** on **Laugavegur 4**, where you'll find handmade jewelry inspired by Iceland's landscapes and the northern lights. The pieces are made from materials like silver and lava stone, giving them a natural, earthy feel. Prices start around **10,000 ISK** for simpler pieces like earrings, and go up to **30,000 ISK** for more elaborate designs.

In the end, if you're after traditional souvenirs, head to **Rammagerðin** at **Skólavörðustígur 12**, where you'll find a wide selection of Viking-themed gifts, local ceramics, and, of course, wool sweaters. Prices for **lopapeysa** sweaters are about **20,000 ISK**, and smaller items like magnets or keychains start around **1,500 ISK**. This is one of the oldest souvenir shops in Reykjavik, so you'll find a lot of variety in one place without having to search all over the city. It's a great stop if you're in a hurry but still want to pick up something meaningful.

3 THE GOLDEN CIRCLE CLASSIC DAY TRIP

3.1 GOLDEN CIRCLE

Y ou have to know that the **Golden Circle** covers around **300 kilometers**, taking you through three of the most important stops in Iceland. **Þingvellir National Park** is the first place you'll visit, and it's where you'll walk between the **North American** and **Eurasian** tectonic plates. The gap between the plates is growing every year, and you can feel that sense of space as you stand in this massive rift valley. This is also where Iceland's parliament, **Alþingi**, was established over a thousand years ago, making it the birthplace of the country's political history. You're not just seeing a park here, but one of the most historically significant places in Iceland.

After Þingvellir, you drive to **Gullfoss**, one of the most powerful waterfalls in the country. The water comes directly from **Langjökull**, the second-largest glacier in Iceland, and plunges down two levels into a deep canyon. When you get close, you'll feel the mist on your face and hear the roar of the water. The energy is incredible, and the sheer force of it makes you realize the power of the natural world here.

Gullfoss is massive, and watching that amount of water fall into the gorge gives you a sense of scale that photos just can't capture.

From there, you head to the **Geysir** geothermal area, where the ground feels alive under your feet. The original **Geysir** doesn't erupt much anymore, but **Strokkur** is active, shooting boiling water up to **30 meters** in the air every few minutes. You'll walk around the area and see bubbling hot springs, steam rising from cracks in the earth, and the constant gurgling of geothermal activity. Every few minutes, Strokkur erupts, and you'll want to be ready with your camera because it happens fast but is always impressive. This spot gives you a close look at the geothermal energy that shapes so much of the landscape in Iceland. It's an intense finish to a route that takes you through some of the most powerful natural features in the country.

3.2 ÞINGVELLIR NATIONAL PARK

In **Þingvellir National Park**, you're standing right between two of the world's biggest tectonic plates, the **North American** and **Eurasian** plates. The ground here is slowly being pulled apart by the forces deep beneath, and you'll see that most clearly when you walk through the **Almannagjá Gorge**, a massive rift that stretches through the park. It's not just a crack in the earth—this gorge is where the land is literally splitting open, and you'll feel the scale of it as you walk between the towering rock walls on either side. The movement of these plates is slow but constant, and it has created a landscape unlike anywhere else.

This is also where **Alþingi**, the country's first parliament, was established in **930 AD**. For centuries, people gathered in this very spot to make laws, resolve disputes, and shape the future of the country. The land has a deep sense of history. When you walk through the park, you're not just seeing natural beauty—you're walking in the footsteps of the early settlers who gathered here to create the political foundation of the country. The mix of geology and history makes this place more than just a scenic stop. It's the heart of the country, where natural forces and human decisions have shaped the land and its people for over a thousand years.

As you move through the park, you'll see cracks and fissures everywhere, some filled with the clearest glacial water you'll ever see. The landscape is rugged and wide open, with **Thingvallavatn**, the largest natural lake, spreading out in the distance. It's a place where you can see both the power of nature and the weight of history all around you, with every step taking you deeper into the story of the land. The beauty is stark, but the sense of significance is what makes **Þingvellir** stand out.

3.3 GULLFOSS WATERFALL

When you get to **Gullfoss**, the first thing that hits you is the sheer force of the water. The **Hvítá River** flows towards the canyon and drops over two massive tiers, first falling **11 meters**, then plunging another **21 meters** into the deep gorge below. You'll hear the power of it before you even see it, and when you get close, the water seems to explode into the canyon with so much force, you can almost feel the ground shake beneath you. The mist fills the air around you, and if you're standing near the edge, you'll feel it soaking through, but that's what makes this place special—you don't just watch Gullfoss, you feel it.

From the **upper platform**, you can stand back and take in the full scale of it. The river winds through the open landscape before it crashes down, and from up here, you see how the waterfall fits into the massive, raw landscape around it. The view is wide, and you see the entire scene laid out, but that's just the beginning.

To truly experience **Gullfoss**, you'll walk down to the **lower platform**, where you're right next to the falls. Here, the power of the water hits you harder. The sound is overwhelming, the spray from the falls is thick, and you'll be standing so close, it feels like the water could reach out and pull you into the rush. The rocks around you are slick from the constant mist, and you'll probably get soaked, but that's part of the experience—the sheer energy of the falls up close is something you won't forget. This view shows you the force and the speed of the water in a way that's impossible to grasp from a distance.

Both views matter. From the top, you see the size, the grandeur. From below, you feel the raw power of it. **Gullfoss** isn't just beautiful; it's powerful, and the closer you get, the more you feel that strength pushing against you. It's a reminder of how wild and unstoppable nature can be.

3.4 THE GEYSIR GEOTHERMAL AREA

When you step into the **Geysir Geothermal Area**, you'll immediately feel the heat rising from the ground. The air is thick with steam, and the smell of sulfur hangs all around. The star of the area is **Strokkur**, and you'll see it erupt every **5 to 10 minutes**, sending boiling water shooting up to **30 meters** in the air. It happens quickly and without much warning, so when the water suddenly bursts up, you feel the power behind it. The timing is unpredictable, but it's frequent enough that you'll catch it multiple times if you stay a bit.

As you walk through the area, you'll notice the ground constantly bubbling. The **hot springs** are active, with water and steam coming out of cracks and pools all over the place. The earth here is full of color —bright reds, oranges, and yellows from the minerals mixing in with the water. The paths take you close enough to feel the steam but keep you at a safe distance because the pools are dangerously hot, reaching temperatures well above boiling. The heat from the ground is intense, and you can see it in the way the water boils and the steam rises constantly from every part of the area.

Strokkur is the main attraction, and each time it erupts, it feels just as impressive. The water shoots up in a straight column, and if the wind is right, you'll get sprayed with a fine mist. But it's not just Strokkur that makes this place feel alive. The entire area is full of geothermal activity—you can hear the boiling water, feel the heat on your face, and see the steam drifting across the landscape. It's an active place, with the earth showing its power right in front of you.

3.5 HIDDEN GEMS ALONG THE GOLDEN CIRCLE

As you move along the **Golden Circle**, there are a few places you shouldn't miss, even though most people do. **Brúarfoss** is one of them. It's off the main route, and it takes about **30 minutes** to walk there, but once you arrive, the view is worth it. The water is **bright blue**, and the falls aren't as big as Gullfoss, but the color and calm make it a special place. You'll be standing on a small bridge that crosses the river, right over the waterfall, and it's often quiet with few people around, so you can enjoy the scene without feeling rushed.

Another spot you should visit is the **Secret Lagoon** in **Flúðir**. It's a natural hot spring, much more relaxed and less crowded than the Blue Lagoon. The **water stays warm year-round**, heated by geothermal energy. You can sit in the water, surrounded by steam rising from the ground, and watch small geysers erupt nearby. It's simple, not flashy, but that's what makes it feel authentic. You're here to relax in the warmth and let the world slow down for a while.

Not far from Gullfoss, there's **Faxi Waterfall**, a smaller, quieter spot that often gets overlooked. It has a **fish ladder** where you can some-times see salmon swimming upstream during the season. It's peaceful, with fewer visitors, and there's a perfect spot for a picnic or just a moment to enjoy the view. The falls may not be as tall, but the setting makes it a great place to stop, especially if you want to escape the busier spots.

One hidden gem that's completely different is **Gjábakkahellir**, a lava tube near **Þingvellir**. This cave was formed by flowing lava, and walking inside feels like stepping into another world. The **walls are rough and jagged**, shaped by the cooling lava, and it's quiet and dark inside, giving you a real sense of Iceland's volcanic landscape. It's not marked like the major tourist spots, so it feels like a discovery when you find it. Exploring the cave gives you a deeper connection to the land, away from the usual sights.

3.6 PRACTICAL GOLDEN CIRCLE ITINERARY

You need to leave **Reykjavik** around **8:00 AM** to make the most of your day. The first stop is **Þingvellir National Park**, about **45 minutes** away. Spend **1 to 1.5 hours** there. Walk through **Almannagjá Gorge**, where the tectonic plates are pulling apart. You can feel the weight of the history in the air—this is where **Alþingi**, the first parliament, was founded. Don't rush, but don't stay too long. You'll need time to explore everything else, and this is just the beginning.

Next, drive **50 minutes** to **Geysir Geothermal Area**. Spend about **45 minutes** here, keeping your eyes on **Strokkur**. It erupts every **5 to 10 minutes**, sending water up to **30 meters** into the air. Walk around and take in the steam rising from the ground and the hot pools bubbling away. This is raw geothermal energy, and you'll feel it. But keep moving—there's more to see.

From there, it's a quick **10-minute** drive to **Gullfoss Waterfall**. You'll want to spend around **45 minutes** here. Start at the upper viewing platform for a sweeping view of the falls, then head down to the lower platform where you'll feel the mist on your face. The sound of the water crashing down is unforgettable. Take it all in, but don't get stuck—you still have time to find some quieter spots.

If you're ahead of schedule, stop at **Faxi Waterfall**, about **15 minutes** from Gullfoss. You won't need more than **20 to 30 minutes** here. It's smaller, but you'll have the place almost to yourself. The peaceful sound of the water and the fish ladder next to it make it a perfect short break. You're not here to rush, but don't linger too long— you've got one more hidden gem to see.

On the way back, if you have time, head toward **Brúarfoss**. It's a bit out of the way, and you'll need to walk about **30 minutes** from the parking area, but the sight of the blue water is worth it. You'll likely have it to yourself, and the color of the water makes this stop feel almost magical.

By the time you're on the road back to **Reykjavik**, it'll be late afternoon or early evening. You'll have seen the most important sights, managed your time well, and discovered a few hidden gems along the way.

3.7 WHERE TO EAT ALONG THE GOLDEN CIRCLE

When you're driving the **Golden Circle**, stop at **Friðheimar**. You'll be eating in a greenhouse surrounded by tomato plants, and their main dish is **fresh tomato soup**, served with warm bread, which is unlimited. The soup is full of flavor, and the atmosphere is unique. They also offer tomato-based drinks, and everything feels fresh, right from the plants. It's close to **Geysir**, so it fits easily into your route.

Next, head to **Efstidalur II**, a family-run farm that serves food straight from their land. Their **beef burgers** are made from their own cattle, and the ice cream is made from their dairy cows. You can see the cows while you eat, through a large window in the dining room. The freshness is clear in every bite, and the food is hearty and satisfying. It's an easy stop between **Geysir** and **Gullfoss**.

In **Laugarvatn**, stop at **Lindin Restaurant**. The dishes focus on fresh, local ingredients, like **Arctic char** or **lamb**. The meals are simple but full of flavor, and the view of the lake adds to the experience. Everything here is well-prepared, and the fish is always a good choice.

For something different, **Minilik Ethiopian Restaurant** near **Selfoss** is a good choice. They serve flavorful dishes like **injera** with various stews. The portions are large, and the food is rich in spices and taste, offering something unique along the route.

Finally, **Héraðsskólinn Restaurant** in **Laugarvatn** gives you a quiet spot to enjoy dishes made from local ingredients. The **lamb stew** is a favorite, and the **rhubarb pie** is the perfect finish. It's a great stop if you're looking for something fresh and comforting before you continue your drive.

Each of these places gives you a taste of the region, focusing on local ingredients and fresh flavors, making them perfect stops along the **Golden Circle**.

4 HVERAGERÐI AND THE SOUTH COAST GATEWAY

4.1 HVERAGERÐI

Hveragerði is a place where you can feel the earth's power as soon as you arrive. The steam rises from the ground, and you can see it all around you. This town sits on top of a geothermal hotspot, and that means the land is alive with **hot springs, steaming vents, and bubbling mud pools**. Everything here revolves around the geothermal activity. You're not just visiting a town; you're stepping into a place where the ground is constantly shifting, where the heat beneath the surface shapes daily life.

The best part of **Hveragerði** is that you can experience these natural forces up close. In the **Geothermal Park**, you'll find boiling water and mud pools right at your feet, and you can even try cooking bread underground, using the earth's heat. It's a simple but unique way to connect with the power beneath the surface, and it's something you won't experience anywhere else.

If you're up for more, you should hike to **Reykjadalur Valley**. It's an easy hike, taking about **45 minutes to an hour**, and at the end, you'll find a **natural hot river** where you can sit and soak. There are no built-up facilities—just the river, warmed by the earth, surrounded by mountains. The water flows through the valley, and you can find your own spot to relax in the heat. The hike is beautiful, with views of the hills and more geothermal areas along the way, and it's the perfect way to unwind in a setting that feels untouched.

Hveragerði also takes full advantage of the geothermal energy with its **greenhouses**. These aren't just for show—they grow fresh vegetables, fruits, and even tropical plants all year round. You can visit these greenhouses and see how the heat from the earth makes it possible to grow produce even when the air outside is cold. It's a clear example of how the town uses what's naturally available to create something sustainable and productive.

4.2 REYKJADALUR HOT SPRINGS

To reach **Reykjadalur Hot Springs**, you'll begin in **Hveragerði**, which is about a **40-minute drive from Reykjavik**. The trailhead is located just a short drive from the town center, and you'll find free parking at the starting point. There's no entrance fee or cost to hike the trail or soak in the hot springs—it's all completely free and open to the public at any time. However, it's best to go during daylight hours, as the trail can be challenging to navigate in the dark.

The hike takes around **45 minutes to an hour** each way, depending on your pace, and starts with a noticeable uphill climb. The path is well-marked and easy to follow, and while it's not difficult, you'll feel the incline early on. As you hike, you'll notice the steam rising from geothermal vents along the way, a reminder of the activity beneath your feet. The landscape opens up, giving you views of the valley below, and the sulfur smell in the air increases as you get closer to the hot river.

Once you arrive at **Reykjadalur**, you'll see the **hot river** running through the valley, with steam rising from the water. The further you walk upstream, the warmer the water gets, so take your time to find a comfortable spot to soak. There are no changing facilities, so be prepared to change near the riverbank. The water is naturally heated, and it feels incredibly relaxing after the hike. You can choose your spot along the river, where the water is the perfect temperature for you.

There's no time limit on how long you can stay, so enjoy the peaceful surroundings and the natural warmth of the river. When you're ready to head back, the hike is mostly downhill, making it quicker and easier than the way up. The entire experience, from the hike to the soak in the hot river, is a chance to immerse yourself in the natural geothermal beauty of the area. There are no specific opening or closing hours, but daylight is recommended for a safe hike.

4.3 BEGINNING THE SOUTH COAST DAY

As you move along the **South Coast**, your first stop is **Seljalandsfoss**, a waterfall that stands at **60 meters high**. What makes this place stand out is that you can actually walk behind the water. The trail takes you right under the cascading falls, so close that you feel the mist on your skin and hear the deep roar of the water as it tumbles down in front of you. The ground behind the waterfall is wet and can get slippery, so take your time as you make your way around. But once you're behind the falls, it's like stepping into another world. You're looking out through a curtain of water, with the landscape stretching beyond, and it's an experience that puts you right in the middle of the natural forces at play here. The views both behind and in front of the falls are equally impressive, but the feeling of standing under that wall of water is something you really can't miss. It's not just about seeing it—you're *in it*.

Next, you'll find **Skógafoss**, one of the most powerful waterfalls along the coast. This one is wider, about **25 meters across**, and the force of the water hitting the ground below is immense. You can walk right up to the base of the waterfall, and as you get closer, you'll be surrounded by the mist that constantly rises from the crashing water. On sunny days, this mist often creates rainbows that seem to hover right in front of you, adding to the magic of the place. **Skógafoss** is much more than just a pretty sight—it's raw power that you can feel as you stand at its base. The spray covers you, the sound is overwhelming, and there's a sense that you're standing at the edge of something much bigger. There's also a long staircase along the side of the waterfall, and if you're willing to make the climb, the view from the top is incredible. From up there, you'll see the river flowing calmly before it plunges over the edge, and beyond that, the vast landscape stretching toward the ocean. The view is wide and open, giving you a whole new perspective on the falls.

Finally, head to **Reynisfjara Beach**, where the black sand stretches out under your feet, and the crashing waves of the Atlantic pound against the shore. What makes this place so unique is the **basalt columns** that rise up along the cliffs. They form these sharp, geometric shapes that look almost too perfect to be natural, but they're the result of volcanic activity that shaped the entire area. You can stand by the columns, feeling the rough texture of the rock, and then turn toward the water where the **Reynisdrangar sea stacks** rise out of the ocean like tall, jagged fingers reaching up toward the sky. The waves here are strong and dangerous, so you need to be careful near the water, but the beauty of the beach is in its wildness. It's not calm or serene—**Reynisfjara** feels like nature in its most untamed form. The black sand against the white foam of the waves, the towering basalt cliffs, and the wind sweeping across the beach all come together to create a scene that feels almost otherworldly.

4.4 GLACIER ADVENTURES NEAR VÍK

To visit **Sólheimajökull Glacier**, you need to be with a guide. This is not a place you can safely go alone, no matter how tempting it looks. The glacier is constantly moving, and it hides deep crevasses, some of which are covered by snow or look like solid ice until you're right up close. A guide knows exactly where to take you, ensuring every step is on firm, safe ground. They will equip you with **crampons**, those metal spikes you attach to your boots so you don't slip on the ice, and an **ice axe**, which helps you keep your balance, especially when the terrain gets steeper.

The walk usually takes about **2 to 3 hours**, and you'll find it's more than just walking on ice. It's a journey into a completely different world, one made entirely of snow, ice, and the slow, almost unnoticeable movement of the glacier beneath your feet. The guide leads you past deep **crevasses**, some of which are so narrow and deep that you'll feel a chill just looking into them. The ice formations, some jagged and sharp, others smooth and almost transparent, show you how the glacier is alive, shifting, and reshaping itself constantly.

As you make your way across the glacier, you'll hear the crunch of the ice under your boots, and with each step, you feel the weight of the ice beneath you. It's cold, but not unbearable if you're dressed correctly. **Wear layers**—the temperature up here is much colder than below, and even on a sunny day, the wind can cut through you. A **waterproof jacket and pants** are crucial because not only are you walking on ice, but the snow can also get wet, especially around the edges of the glacier where the melt begins.

Every now and then, the guide will stop to explain what's happening underneath the ice. They'll show you how the glacier is slowly retreating, how the black volcanic ash that covers parts of the ice was left behind by past eruptions, and how the crevasses form as the glacier moves and shifts. You'll see the blue ice up close, and it's unlike anything you've seen before—it's not just cold, it looks cold, almost as if the ice is glowing from within. The **blue color** comes from the weight of the ice pressing out the air bubbles, and it creates a depth that makes the ice feel like it's alive.

As you walk, the guide will keep a close eye on everyone, assuring you're walking safely, using your crampons properly, and keeping a steady pace. It's important to trust the guide's instructions, especially when navigating more challenging sections. You might have to walk along ridges or cross small crevasses, and this is where the **ice axe** becomes essential to keep your balance.

4.5 HIDDEN SOUTH COAST GEMS

If you want something quieter and off the beaten path along the **South Coast**, start with **Kvernufoss**. It's close to **Skógafoss**, but you won't find the same crowds. To get there, park at the **Skógar Museum** and take the **20-minute trail** that leads into a narrow gorge. The waterfall itself is **30 meters high**, and you can walk behind it, giving you a unique view that most visitors miss. The best part is, it's free, open year-round, and you'll often have it to yourself. Make sure to wear waterproof gear because you'll get close enough to feel the mist, especially if you want to enjoy the view from behind the falls.

For something more interesting, head to the **Sólheimasandur Plane Wreck**. The wreck is the remains of a **US Navy DC-3** that crashed in **1973**, now sitting on a desolate black sand beach. You won't find this on a lot of tour guides. There's no official parking lot, but you'll see a small area off the **Ring Road** near **Sólheimajökull Glacier**, where you can leave your car and start the **45-minute walk** each way. The walk itself is easy, but the wide-open black sand makes it feel like you're crossing another planet. When you finally reach the wreckage, the contrast of the twisted metal against the dark sand and open sky is stunning. It's free to visit and open all day, but if you go early or late in the day, you'll have fewer people around, and the eerie setting will be even more striking.

For a peaceful beach experience, avoid the main tourist spot at **Dyrhólaey** and instead drive further down the road past the **Lighthouse**. Keep going until you find a secluded area of the beach. From here, you'll get an incredible view of the **Dyrhólaey Arch**, and the black sand stretches out in front of you with hardly anyone around. The waves here are strong and dramatic, adding to the wild feeling of the place, but be careful, as they can be unpredictable. The beach is always open, and it's a completely free experience that feels worlds away from the busier parts of the coast.

For a nice hiking, make your way to **Þakgil Canyon**, which is hidden inland from **Vík**. The drive there takes you off the main road onto **Route 214**, a gravel road that gets bumpy, but it's fine for most cars in the summer. Once you arrive, **Þakgil** offers a peaceful, green valley surrounded by steep cliffs and caves. The trails here are less crowded than the ones along the coast, and they take you deep into the mountains for some of the most untouched scenery you'll find. The hiking area is open in summer, and there's no charge for parking or to enter the trails, making it perfect for anyone who wants to escape the crowds and enjoy Iceland's nature in solitude.

Don't miss **Stjórnarfoss**, a small, beautiful waterfall near **Kirkjubæjarklaustur**. It's just a quick detour off the **Ring Road**— follow the signs to the **Klausturhof Guesthouse** and park there. From the parking lot, it's a **5-minute walk** to the waterfall. **Stjórnarfoss** may not be as large as others, but it's peaceful and often overlooked by travelers. It's free to visit, and if you're there in the summer, the pool at the base is great for a quick dip, offering a perfect way to cool down after exploring.

4.6 WHERE TO EAT AND STAY IN THE SOUTH COAST

For the first you have to start with **Hótel Skógar**, located just a few minutes' walk from **Skógafoss** on **Skógarfoss Road**, easily accessible from the **Ring Road**. This small, intimate hotel offers rooms for about **€150 to €200 per night**, depending on the season. The rooms are comfortable with beautiful views of the surrounding mountains and the nearby waterfall. After a day of exploring, you'll want to enjoy dinner at the restaurant. The **lamb stew** is a must-try, made with locally sourced lamb, and the **fish of the day**, often **Arctic char**, is always fresh. Dinner is served from **6:30 PM to 9:30 PM**, and the price for a meal is around **€40 to €50 per person**. It's a small restaurant, so booking ahead is a good idea, especially during peak travel months. While staying here, you can visit **Skógafoss**, which is just a short walk away, or drive to the **Sólheimasandur Plane Wreck**, about a **10-minute drive** down the **Ring Road**.

For a personal, cozy experience, head to **Hrifunes Guesthouse**, about **20 minutes from Kirkjubæjarklaustur** on **Road 209**. You'll feel right at home here, with rooms priced around **€120 to €160 per night**. The guesthouse is family-run, and the highlight is the communal dinner they serve every evening at **7 PM**. For around **€40 per person**, you'll enjoy a family-style meal made from fresh, local ingredients, including **Icelandic lamb**, **root vegetables**, and homemade desserts. The food here is simple but full of flavor, and it's served in a warm, friendly environment where you can chat with other guests about your day's adventures. Around the area, you can visit **Fjaðrárgljúfur Canyon**, a **30-minute drive** from the guesthouse, or relax in the peaceful countryside, taking in the views.

For something more upscale, **Fosshotel Glacier Lagoon** is the perfect choice, located on **Hnappavellir** between **Jökulsárlón** and **Skaftafell**. This modern hotel offers rooms from **€200 to €300 per night**, with large windows that give you stunning views of the ocean or mountains. The restaurant is more high-end, serving dinner from **6 PM to 10 PM**, with prices around **€60 to €80 per person**. The **slow-cooked lamb** is one of their specialties, incredibly tender and rich, and the **Arctic char** is also a standout, light and perfectly cooked. Be sure to make a reservation, as this is a popular spot for those traveling between the glaciers. While staying here, you're in the perfect location to visit **Jökulsárlón Glacier Lagoon**, about **30 minutes** away, or go hiking in **Skaftafell National Park**, just a **20-minute drive**.

For a casual and down-to-earth, stop at **Gamla Fjósið** near **Hvolsvöllur**, located on **Road 249**, about a **10-minute drive from Seljalandsfoss**. This restaurant is housed in an old barn, and the prices are reasonable, with **beef burgers** made from farm-raised meat costing around **€15**. The atmosphere is rustic, and the food is simple but delicious, with fresh ingredients from the surrounding farm. Make sure to save room for dessert—the **Icelandic Skyr** and homemade cakes are a real treat. They're open from **11 AM to 9 PM**, so it's a great place to stop for lunch or dinner while you're on the road. If you're heading to **Seljalandsfoss** or **Gljúfrabúi**, this is the perfect spot to grab a meal before or after your visit.

For a quieter, more secluded stay near **Vík**, consider **Vík Cottages**. These small cottages, located just a short walk from **Reynisfjara Beach**, offer a peaceful retreat with rates around **€150 per night**. Each cottage comes with a kitchenette, so you can prepare your own meals if you want, but if you prefer to eat out, head into **Vík** to **Halldórskaffi**. It's a cozy café with simple dishes like **lamb soup** and fresh fish. Prices for a meal here range from **€15 to €30**, and they're open from **12 PM to 9 PM**. The atmosphere is relaxed, and it's a great place to sit and unwind after a day of exploring **Reynisfjara Beach** or the **Dyrhólaey Peninsula**, both of which are within a **10 to 15-minute drive** from the cottages.

5 VÍK Í MÝRDAL A SEASIDE VILLAGE

5.1 INTRODUCTION

When you get to **Vík**, the first thing you'll notice is the **black sand beach** stretching out in front of you, unlike anything you've seen before. It's not your typical beach; the sand is made from volcanic ash, and it has this deep, dark color that makes the whole area feel dramatic. The waves here are rough, constantly crashing onto the shore, and you can feel the power of the Atlantic Ocean as you stand there, looking out at the water. The black sand, the roaring waves, and the towering **Reynisdrangar sea stacks** rising out of the ocean give the place a mystical, almost haunting atmosphere. These sea stacks, made of basalt, are striking because they stand tall, like natural pillars, just off the shore. The local legend says they're trolls who were caught in the sunlight and turned to stone, adding a bit of magic to the already stunning view.

Vík is a small village, but don't let that fool you. The beauty surrounding it is immense. As you walk around, you'll see the colorful houses scattered across the landscape, with green hills behind them and the black beach ahead. The homes add a touch of brightness to the darker tones of the beach and mountains. One of the best spots to get a view of the entire area is from **Vík Church**, which sits on a hill over-looking the village. The church itself is simple—a white building with a red roof—but the view is something else. From up there, you can see the entire coastline, the beach stretching endlessly in one direction, and the mountains rising in the other. It's quiet, and it feels like you've found a hidden spot where you can take in all of Vík's beauty without any distractions.

What really makes **Vík** stand out, though, is the feeling of being surrounded by nature in its rawest form. You have the sea on one side, with the dark beach and crashing waves, and the mountains on the other, rising steeply from the village. There's a sense that this place has been shaped by the elements over centuries, and when you're here, you're right in the middle of it. The beach, **Reynisfjara**, is not just a place to take pictures—it's a place where you can feel the power of nature. The waves are strong and unpredictable, so it's important to keep your distance from the water's edge, but standing there, with the sound of the ocean all around you and the sight of the **basalt columns** lining the cliffs, you really feel connected to the wildness of the landscape.

5.2 REYNISFJARA BEACH AND DYRHÓLAEY CLIFFS

When you go to **Reynisfjara Beach**, the first thing that hits you is how completely different it feels from any beach you've ever seen. The **black sand** isn't just dark—it's made from volcanic ash, and it stretches out endlessly in front of you, disappearing into the horizon.

You'll notice immediately how the ocean feels more alive here, with the waves crashing powerfully against the shore, sending sprays of saltwater high into the air. The wind is often strong, and you can taste the salt on your lips as you take in the raw beauty of this place. But while you're mesmerized by the sights and sounds, you need to keep in mind that these waves are unpredictable. **Sneaker waves** are a real danger here—big waves that surge up the beach out of nowhere, so always stay far back from the water. Even on calm days, this ocean is not one to be underestimated.

As you walk along the beach, your eyes will be drawn to the **Reynisdrangar sea stacks**, rising straight out of the ocean like ancient towers. These basalt pillars stand at about **66 meters** tall and are one of the most iconic features of the beach. There's a local legend about these sea stacks being trolls, caught by the sunlight and turned to stone as they tried to pull a ship to shore. It's easy to see why stories like that have grown around them—they have a mystical, almost eerie presence. Standing there, with the sea pounding at their bases, they look immovable, as if they've been standing guard over this coastline for centuries.

Keep walking toward the cliffs, and you'll see something just as incredible: the **basalt columns** at the base of **Reynisfjall Mountain**. These columns are unlike anything else you'll see on this coast. The lava that formed them cooled in such a way that it created these almost perfect hexagonal shapes, stacked one on top of the other like a natural staircase. As you stand in front of them, you'll realize how precise and geometric they look—nature's architecture at its finest. You can even climb a few of the lower columns, and from there, you'll get a better view of the beach and the cliffs towering above. The columns are one of the most photographed spots on the beach for good reason—they add a layer of uniqueness to this already dramatic landscape.

Meanwhile you visit, don't forget to look up. The cliffs above

Reynisfjara are home to thousands of seabirds, including the famous **puffins**. These birds nest in the cliffs during the summer, from **May to August**, and their colorful beaks and clumsy flight make them a favorite among visitors. If you're lucky, you'll see them swooping down to the ocean, diving for fish, and then returning to their nests high above. Watching them fly back and forth between the sea and their nests gives you a sense of how alive this place is—nature is all around you here, and it feels vibrant and wild.

A short drive away from **Reynisfjara**, you'll reach the **Dyrhólaey Cliffs**, and the first thing you'll notice as you make your way up the winding road is the sheer sense of space and scale that opens up before you. At the top, you'll find yourself looking out over miles and miles of black sand beaches, the waves crashing far below. One of the most striking features here is the **Dyrhólaey Arch**, a massive stone arch that juts out into the ocean. The waves have carved it over thousands of years, and on calm days, small boats can actually pass through it. Standing at the edge of the cliffs, looking out at the arch, you'll feel the wind pulling at your clothes, the sound of the ocean echoing off the rocks—it's a place where nature dominates everything.

From this vantage point, you can also see **Reynisdrangar** in the distance, the sea stacks still standing tall in the ocean. But here, at **Dyrhólaey**, the cliffs drop dramatically into the water below, and the views stretch as far as your eyes can see. The sense of being on the edge of the world is strong here, especially with the endless horizon of the Atlantic stretching out before you.

Just like at **Reynisfjara**, the cliffs at **Dyrhólaey** are alive with birdlife. **Puffins** nest here too, and if you visit between **May and August**, you'll see them dotting the grassy cliffs, their bright beaks standing out against the green. They fly back and forth between the ocean and their nests, and you can watch them dive into the water to catch fish. The best part about watching the puffins here is how close you can get without disturbing them—the cliffs offer perfect viewing points, and you don't have to go far to see them in action.

5.3 VISIT NEARBY GLACIERS

To visit **Sólheimajökull Glacier**, you need to head west from **Vík** along the **Ring Road**. The turnoff to **Road 221** is easy to spot, and once you're on that road, you'll drive directly to the parking lot in about **5 minutes**. From the parking area, it's just a short **10-15 minute walk** to reach the glacier's edge, where you'll immediately be struck by the rugged, icy surface. The landscape changes quickly as you move away from the more typical South Coast sights. The glacier itself is like a frozen river of ice that you can see stretching into the distance, with cracks and deep blue ice visible right in front of you.

The best and safest way to experience the glacier is through a **guided glacier hike**. Trying to explore on your own is dangerous because of hidden crevasses and other hazards. Guides provide all the equipment you need, like **crampons** and an **ice axe**, and they know the glacier well enough to navigate its changing landscape. The tours cost about **€80 to €120** per person and usually last around **2.5 to 4 hours**. These hikes take you deep into the glacier, where you can actually touch the ancient ice, peer into crevasses, and walk safely on the slippery surface. You'll feel the cold air rising from the glacier as your guide explains how the glacier has been shaped by centuries of volcanic activity and weather patterns.

For something more thrilling, you can try **ice climbing**. These tours cost a little more, around **€150**, but they're a completely different experience. You'll use ropes and technical gear to climb vertical ice walls, feeling the full weight of the glacier beneath you. It's hard work, but nothing compares to standing at the top of an ice wall, surrounded by the stillness and beauty of the glacier.

Sólheimajökull is open year-round, but the tours are most popular

47

in the summer when the weather is a little more predictable, and the days are long. Winter visits offer a chance to see **ice caves**, which form naturally beneath the glacier. These caves are stunning, with walls of blue ice that seem to glow from within. Ice cave tours start around **€150 to €200**, and it's something you won't want to miss if you're visiting in the colder months.

If you want to take your glacier adventure even further, consider a **snowmobile tour** on the larger **Mýrdalsjökull** ice cap above **Sólheimajökull**. These tours cost more, about **€250 to €300**, but they give you the chance to ride across the glacier, seeing the vast, frozen expanse from a completely different perspective. The views from the glacier are incredible—you can see mountains and valleys stretching out in all directions.

I suggest you to dress warmly, with layers, because the glacier can be freezing even on warmer days. Trust me! Wear a waterproof jacket and sturdy boots, and don't forget gloves and a hat. **Sólheimajökull** is a living glacier, constantly shifting and changing, and walking on it gives you a sense of just how powerful nature can be.

5.4 HIDDEN TRAILS AROUND VÍK

Hjörleifshöfði, often referred to because of its famous **Yoda Cave**, is just a short drive about **15 minutes east of Vík**, and it's an ideal spot for a quieter hike. The path is about **4.5 kilometers round trip**, and it takes around **two hours** to complete, making it accessible for most people while still providing an immersive experience. You'll start by walking across a vast, open plain of black sand that stretches out before you like something from another world. It's volcanic in origin, and as you walk, the deep silence of the area will make you feel like you're far from the busier spots along the coast.

The highlight of the hike is the climb up **Hjörleifshöfði**, a hill with views that go on forever once you reach the top. From up there, you can see the dramatic coast on one side and the endless stretch of black sand plains on the other. The views are open and vast, and on a clear day, you can see for miles. What makes this hike unique, aside from the views, is the **Yoda Cave**, which sits at the base of the hill. It's a naturally formed cave that looks eerily like the Star Wars character, and exploring it adds a fun, unexpected twist to the hike. The trail is free to access, and it's open year-round, but it's best to go on dry days because the path can get slippery when wet. **This is a spot where you won't run into many people**, making it perfect for those who want solitude and an otherworldly landscape.

For a hike that offers a different perspective on the area, head to **Reynisfjall Mountain**, located just above **Reynisfjara Beach**. This trail is more challenging, but it's a **5-kilometer round trip** hike that takes around **2 to 3 hours** to complete, depending on your pace and how long you spend enjoying the views. **You'll start near the beach and begin your ascent up the mountain**, and while the climb is steep in places, the payoff is worth it. From the top, you'll have sweeping views of the **Reynisdrangar sea stacks** rising out of the ocean below, framed by the black sand beaches that stretch for miles along the coast. The views are different from what you'd see down at the beach itself—here, you get a much wider perspective of the dramatic coast-line and the towering sea stacks, **all without the crowds**.

One important thing to remember is that this trail isn't heavily marked, so **it's a good idea to bring a GPS or map**, especially if the weather is cloudy or foggy. **The hike is free**, and it's best to do it on a clear day when you can fully appreciate the views from the top. **The hike is a little more isolated**, so if you want to avoid the busier spots and still get a dramatic view of the South Coast, this is a great option.

For a longer, more adventurous trail, head to **Þakgil Valley**, about **30 minutes northeast of Vík**. **This hike is around 10 kilometers round trip** and takes about **4 to 5 hours**, so it's best suited for those who want to spend a good part of the day hiking and exploring the quieter parts of the South Coast. The trail leads you through a stunning valley surrounded by steep cliffs, and along the way, you'll pass rivers and waterfalls that feel almost untouched by people. What makes this hike unique is the sense of isolation—you're surrounded by nature, and there's a good chance you won't run into anyone else while you're out on the trail. **There's a small campsite at the start of the trail**, so if you're feeling adventurous, you could even plan an overnight stay. This area is only accessible from **June to September**, so be sure to check the weather and trail conditions before heading out. There's no fee to hike this trail, but **you'll want to be prepared with good hiking boots and plenty of water**, as the trail is more challenging than some of the others around Vík.

If you're looking for a shorter, easier hike, check out **Fjaðrárgljúfur Canyon**, located about **45 minutes east of Vík**. This hike is just **2 kilometers round trip**, and it takes under an hour to complete, but what it lacks in length, it more than makes up for in beauty. The canyon walls rise up steeply on either side, and the river winds its way through the bottom of the canyon, creating a serene and peaceful setting. **As you walk along the edge of the canyon**, you'll be able to stop at several viewpoints where you can take in the full scope of the cliffs and the lush green landscape below. This trail is perfect if you want a quick but stunning hike that gives you a break from the more crowded areas of the South Coast. **There's no fee to enter**, and the trail is open year-round, but it's especially beautiful in the summer when the canyon is covered in greenery and the river is flowing at its fullest.

5.5 DINING AND ACCOMMODATION

You should definitely go to **Smiðjan Brugghús**. It's right on **Austurvegur 14**, an easy-to-find spot in the center of town. The moment you walk in, you'll feel the relaxed, welcoming atmosphere, and if you're into craft beer, this is the place for you. They brew their own beer on-site, and pairing it with their food is a must. The **Lamburger** is one of the best things on the menu—made from local lamb, it's juicy, full of flavor, and really shows off the quality of Icelandic ingredients. The fries that come with it are perfect, crispy on the outside and soft inside, and they've got several dips to choose from, which adds a nice touch. **It's open daily from 11:00 AM to 10:00 PM**, and for a full meal, expect to spend around **ISK 2,500 to 3,500**. If you're driving, parking is easy and close by, or you can just stroll over if you're staying nearby since it's right in town. **Smiðjan Brugghús** gives you that perfect mix of local flavor and a casual spot to unwind after a busy day.

For a taste of traditional Icelandic dishes, go to **Halldórskaffi**, which is located at **Víkurbraut 28**. You'll feel the cozy, homely vibe as soon as you step in, thanks to the fact that it's set inside an old house. The highlight here is definitely the **plokkfiskur**, a classic Icelandic fish stew made with fresh cod, potatoes, and a creamy sauce that's just perfect on a cold day. The way it's cooked feels like a warm, comforting home meal, something you'd want to enjoy slowly. They also serve **arctic char**, which is another local favorite—light, flaky, and packed with flavor. The whole setting makes you feel like you're experiencing real, authentic Icelandic cooking. **It's open from 11:30 AM to 9:00 PM**, and you can expect to pay about **ISK 2,500 to 4,000** for a meal. It's close to everything in Vík, so walking over from your accommodation is no hassle at all, and if you're driving, there's parking nearby. It's a place where you can relax and enjoy local food without feeling rushed.

If you're in the mood for something quick but don't want to sacrifice quality, head to **The Soup Company** on **Víkurbraut 5**. It's a small place, but it packs a punch when it comes to flavor. Their **Icelandic lamb soup** is fantastic, served in a warm bread bowl that's perfect for dipping. It's hearty and filling, especially if you're looking for something to warm you up. They also offer vegetarian soups and daily specials, so there's always something fresh to try. The price here is reasonable, around **ISK 1,500 to 2,500**, and it's open **from 12:00 PM to 9:00 PM**. Located right in the center of town, it's easy to stop by, whether you're looking for a quick lunch or an early dinner. It's one of those spots where the food is simple but incredibly satisfying, and you won't leave hungry.

As for places to stay, **Hotel Kría**, located at **Sléttuvegur 12**, is one of the top choices if you're looking for comfort with a touch of modern style. The rooms are spacious and clean, with large windows offering views of the nearby mountains or the ocean. It's perfect if you're looking for somewhere to rest and recharge after a day of exploring the area. **Prices start around ISK 20,000 per night**, depending on the season, and it's worth it for the quality and comfort you get. The hotel's restaurant, **Drangar**, is an added bonus. You can enjoy a meal there if you're too tired to venture out, with a menu that features locally sourced ingredients, bringing the taste of Iceland right to your table. It's easy to get to the hotel, with parking available, and it's just a short walk from the main part of town, so everything you need is close by.

If you are on the budget, there's **Puffin Hotel Vík**, located at **Víkurbraut 26**. It's a simple, family-run place, but the rooms are comfortable and clean, with everything you need for a pleasant stay. **Rooms start at around ISK 14,000 per night**, making it a great choice if you're watching your budget but still want a cozy place to stay. The location is ideal, just a short walk from restaurants, shops, and the beach. The staff here are friendly and always happy to help with recommendations, making your stay feel even more welcoming. If you're looking for something affordable and convenient, **Puffin Hotel Vík** gives you exactly that.

In the end, **Vík Cottages**, located on **Sunnubraut 1**, offer something special. These small, individual cottages are perfect if you're traveling as a couple or in a small group and want a bit of privacy.

Each cottage has beautiful views of the surrounding cliffs and the ocean, so you can enjoy the scenery without leaving your doorstep. **Prices start at around ISK 18,000 per night**, and you get a cozy, intimate space with all the essentials. It's just a few minutes' walk from the center of town, but it feels tucked away enough to give you that sense of seclusion and quiet, which is perfect to relax after a long day. Now, let's talk about Höfn in the next chapter.

6 HÖFN GLACIERS AND SEA

6.1 OVERVIEW

Höfn is a small town on the southeastern coast, perfectly placed between the sea and the mountains, and it's really known for two things: **the glaciers and the seafood**. As soon as you get here, you'll feel how calm and quiet the town is, but don't mistake that for it being dull—there's always something happening at the harbor, with the fishing boats bringing in fresh catches every day, especially the famous **langoustine**, which you'll find on almost every restaurant menu. The seafood here is some of the best you'll find, and the local restaurants really know how to prepare it in a way that brings out the rich, fresh flavors of the sea.

This town sits on a **peninsula**, so wherever you walk, you've got the ocean on one side and the towering mountains and glaciers on the other. The whole place feels like it's surrounded by nature, and even though it's small, you can tell it's a key stop for anyone wanting to explore the nearby **Vatnajökull glacier**, which is one of the main reasons people come to Höfn. **The glacier dominates the landscape,** and from the town, you can see its icy peaks in the distance, especially on clear days when the view stretches far beyond the harbor.

One of the first things you'll notice is the harbor itself. It's the heart of Höfn, always busy with fishing boats, and you'll see locals working with the fresh catch of the day. Seafood is a big part of life here, and **langoustine**, which is like a small lobster, is a real specialty. You can't leave Höfn without trying it, whether it's in a simple grilled dish or a creamy soup that really warms you up after a day out exploring. The town even hosts an annual **Lobster Festival**, where locals and visitors gather to celebrate this local delicacy, so if you're lucky enough to be there during the festival, you'll get to enjoy the best of what the town has to offer in terms of food and local culture.

In terms of size, **Höfn is small but well-equipped**. You've got a few restaurants, guesthouses, and cafés where you can relax and enjoy a quiet moment. The town is a great place to stay for a few days, especially if you're planning to explore the nearby glaciers and fjords. It's located right off the **Ring Road**, which makes it easy to get to other destinations along the southeast coast, but it's far enough from the more crowded tourist spots that you'll feel like you're truly away from the hustle and bustle. **The whole place has a laid-back vibe**, perfect if you're looking to slow down and enjoy the scenery.

You'll find that **the connection between the town and its natural surroundings** is what really sets Höfn apart. The way the glaciers rise up in the background and the calm waters of the harbor stretch out in front of you, it feels like the town is nestled right between two worlds —one of ice and mountains, and the other of the open sea. And because it's smaller and quieter than some of the bigger tourist hubs, you really get a sense of peace here. It's the kind of place where you can walk around and just soak in the beauty of the mountains on one side and the sea on the other, with fishing boats coming and going, adding to the sense that this is a place deeply connected to nature.

The town itself is a great base for exploring **Vatnajökull National**

Park, with plenty of options for glacier tours and hikes. And if you're not up for anything too strenuous, just wandering through town and along the harbor, enjoying the views, gives you a real sense of what makes Höfn so special. The people here are friendly and welcoming, and you'll find that even though it's small, **Höfn has everything you need to make your stay comfortable**—whether that's a cozy guesthouse to rest after a long day, or a café where you can sit and enjoy a coffee while looking out at the mountains.

6.2 VISITING VATNAJÖKULL GLACIER

For the first you have to start by heading to **Skaftafell**, which is about **50 kilometers west of Höfn** along the **Ring Road**. It's a straightforward drive, and you'll be surrounded by incredible scenery the whole way. Once you arrive, the best place to begin is at the **Skaftafell Visitor Center**, which is located at **Skaftafellsvegur 999**. It's open from **9:00 AM to 7:00 PM in summer**, and **10:00 AM to 6:00 PM in winter**, though it's always good to double-check the hours if you're visiting during the off-season. The parking is easy, and it costs about **ISK 750 for the day**.

When you're there, the first thing you'll probably want to do is join a **guided glacier hike**. Walking on the glacier is something you can't do by yourself, so booking a tour is essential. The guides will give you all the gear you need—crampons to grip the ice, ice axes to steady yourself—and they make sure you're safe every step of the way. These hikes are not too difficult, but they do require a bit of fitness since you'll be walking for **3 to 4 hours** across the glacier's surface. The best part is getting to explore the **deep blue crevasses**, which are like cracks in the ice, giving you a look deep into the glacier. **Prices for the hikes start around ISK 12,000 to 15,000 per person**, depending on the company and the length of the hike, but the experience is worth every bit.

For a unique adventure, visit during the winter months, from **November to March**, when you can explore the **ice caves** that form underneath the glacier. These caves are only accessible during the colder months when the ice is stable, and the bright blue walls of the cave make it feel like you're walking through a world made entirely of ice. Most tours to the ice caves start from **Jökulsárlón Glacier Lagoon**, which is about **45 minutes west of Höfn**, right off the Ring Road. When you get there, you'll meet your guide who will take you in a 4x4 closer to the caves before starting the short hike to the entrance. **Ice cave tours cost around ISK 19,000 to 22,000 per person**, and the entire tour lasts about **2.5 to 4 hours**. You won't need to worry about equipment, as your guide will provide everything, including helmets and crampons, but make sure to wear warm clothes since the temperatures inside the caves can drop significantly.

If you want to experience the glacier from a more relaxed perspective, head to **Jökulsárlón Glacier Lagoon** itself. Here, huge chunks of ice break off from the glacier and float gently through the lagoon. The best way to see it all is by hopping on a **boat tour**, which brings you right up to the icebergs. The tours last around **40 minutes** and cost about **ISK 7,000 per person**. It's a slower, peaceful way to take in the grandeur of the glacier, especially if you're not up for the hike but still want to experience its beauty.

For those who prefer to stay on land but still want to explore the glacier's surroundings, the **Svartifoss Waterfall** trail is a perfect hike. The trail is about **5.5 kilometers round trip** and takes **1.5 to 2 hours**, making it accessible for most fitness levels. It's an easy to moderate hike, and along the way, you'll walk through lush greenery before reaching the glacier's edge. While you won't be able to step directly on the ice without a guide, the views are stunning, and it gives you a fantastic look at the sheer size of **Vatnajökull**.

Before you set off for the day, make sure you're well-prepared. **Dress in warm, waterproof layers** because the weather can change quickly, even in summer. Good **hiking boots** are a must, especially if you're doing a glacier walk, and it's always smart to bring a **small backpack with water and snacks** to keep you fueled. The sun reflects off the ice, so you'll definitely want **sunglasses** to protect your eyes from the glare.

When you visit **Vatnajökull**, the sheer size and beauty of the glacier are something you won't forget. For sure! It's the largest ice cap in Europe, and walking on it, seeing its blue crevasses up close, or even stepping into an ice cave will make you realize how powerful nature can be.

6.3 DIAMOND BEACH

Diamond Beach is one of the most surreal places you'll visit because of the way the massive icebergs, which break off from the nearby glacier, get washed up onto the pitch-black volcanic sand. What really stands out is how these chunks of ice, some small and clear like glass, others enormous and glowing blue, contrast with the dark sand beneath them. It's not just the beauty of the ice that makes this place special— it's how it constantly changes. Every time you come here, the shapes, sizes, and even the number of icebergs are different, depending on the tides and how the glacier is shifting. The scene is constantly in motion, and it makes you feel like you're stepping into a natural art gallery, with the icebergs as the stars of the show.

You'll find **Diamond Beach** just off the **Ring Road (Route 1)**, about **80 kilometers west of Höfn**, which is roughly an hour's drive. The location is easy to spot, and there's plenty of **free parking** right near the beach, so you won't need to worry about any entry fees. Once you park, it's only a short walk from your car down to the shoreline, where the black sand meets the ice. The beach is open 24 hours, and while it's beautiful at any time of day, it's especially magical at **sunrise or sunset**. That's when the light hits the ice at the perfect angle, causing it to sparkle and reflect a range of colors that you won't see anywhere else.

As soon as you step onto the sand, you'll see the **icebergs scattered across the shore**. Some are small enough that you could hold them in your hand, though they'll start melting as soon as you touch them, and others are taller than you, almost like small ice sculptures that nature has carved out. The **textures of the ice** vary too—some pieces are perfectly smooth, while others are jagged and rough, with deep blue hues that look almost unreal. Walking along the beach, you'll get to see the full range of sizes and shapes, and because the beach stretches out quite a bit, there's plenty of room to explore.

As you walk, you can hear the waves crashing and watch as new pieces of ice are gently pushed ashore by the water. The **movement of the waves** brings life to the scene, constantly reshaping how the ice sits on the beach. It's a great place for **photography**, especially because of the way the bright ice contrasts with the dark sand. If you've got a camera, you'll find endless opportunities to capture stunning shots from different angles, whether it's close-ups of the ice formations or wide shots of the beach stretching out with the icebergs scattered across the sand.

While you're enjoying the beach, just make sure to be cautious around the water. The **waves can come in fast**, and the icebergs, while beautiful, can be dangerous if they shift unexpectedly, especially if they're large and still floating. It's best to admire them from a little distance and always be mindful of where the tide is. This beach is wild and untouched, and that's part of what makes it so special. There are no shops, no cafés—just the **natural beauty of the ocean, the sand, and the ice**.

Visiting **Diamond Beach** is more about soaking in the experience rather than ticking off activities from a list. It's a place where you can slow down and just watch as the waves roll in, bringing in fresh pieces of ice, while others slowly melt back into the sea. The contrast between the **bright, sparkling icebergs and the dark volcanic sand** is something you won't find anywhere else, and the way the scenery changes from day to day, hour to hour, keeps it fresh and exciting every time you visit.

There's no rush here, no need to move on quickly. Whether you spend just an hour or linger for longer, **Diamond Beach** will leave a lasting impression with its peaceful atmosphere and striking natural beauty.

6.4 WHERE TO STAY AND EAT

The best way to dive into the local flavor is to start with **Pakkhús Restaurant**. It's right by the harbor at **Kaffivegur 3**, so you're eating fresh seafood practically straight from the ocean. This place is all about the **grilled langoustine**, which is served with garlic butter that's just perfect—rich but not overwhelming, letting the sweetness of the langoustine really shine through. You're going to want to savor every bite because this is exactly what Höfn is famous for. **Prices** for a meal here range from **ISK 4,000 to 6,500**, depending on how much langoustine you're ready to dive into, and they're open every day from **11:30 AM to 9:30 PM**, which gives you plenty of time to stop by for either lunch or dinner. Now, if you're someone with a sweet tooth, don't skip dessert here. Their **Skyr cake** is something special—it's light, creamy, and made from Iceland's traditional Skyr, which is kind of like a yogurt-cheese hybrid. It's not heavy, just the right touch after all that rich seafood.

If you're looking for something a little more upscale, head over to **Humarhöfnin**, located at **Hafnarbraut 4**. This place is well known for its elegant seafood dishes, but again, the **langoustine tails** steal the show. They're grilled to perfection, usually served with sides that rotate based on what's fresh and in season, often with roasted vegetables or buttery potatoes. It's a bit pricier than Pakkhús, with meals costing between **ISK 5,000 and 7,500 per person**, but the quality and presentation make it worth every krona. They're open from **12:00 PM to 9:00 PM** during the summer season, and the atmosphere is always warm and welcoming, making it a perfect spot for a leisurely dinner after a day of exploring the area. If you've saved room for dessert, I'd recommend trying their **homemade ice cream**. It's nothing fancy, just smooth and rich, but it's the perfect way to end a meal that's already so full of flavors.

For a more casual and laid-back option, you can't go wrong with **Z Bistro**. Located at **Hafnarbraut 11**, this bistro is the kind of place where you can pop in for something simple but still full of flavor. The menu includes classics like **fish and chips** and pizza, so if you're traveling with a group that has mixed tastes, this place is ideal. You'll be looking at **ISK 2,500 to 4,500** per person, making it one of the more affordable spots in town. They're open from **11:00 AM to 10:00 PM**, so you can stop by pretty much anytime. Now, if you're craving something sweet to round out your meal, their **chocolate mousse** is the way to go—it's rich but not too heavy, with just the right amount of sweetness.

Now, when it comes to **where to stay**, if you want something central and straightforward, **Höfn Guesthouse** at **Vikurbraut 20** is a great choice. It's simple, clean, and comfortable, with everything you need for a good night's rest after a long day of sightseeing. The **rooms** here are priced between **ISK 15,000 and 25,000** per night, depending on the season and room type, and **check-in** starts at **3:00 PM**. What's nice about this guesthouse is that it's within walking distance of all the main restaurants and shops, so you won't need to drive around much while you're staying here. It's perfect for travelers who want convenience without sacrificing comfort.

For something a little more luxurious, consider **Hotel Höfn**, located at **Vikurbraut 13**. This hotel is known for its spacious rooms, and some even offer stunning views of the surrounding glaciers, making it a perfect spot if you want to relax in style. The rooms are priced between **ISK 20,000 and 35,000** per night, again depending on the season and room choice. The hotel is open year-round, and what's nice is that they also have an in-house restaurant, **Ósinn**, where you can enjoy even more local seafood if you don't feel like venturing out.

Finally, if you're on a budget, **Höfn Hostel** at **Hafnarbraut 8** is a solid option. It's simple and no-frills, but it's got everything you need —clean rooms, friendly staff, and a convenient location. **Prices** here range from **ISK 8,000 to 15,000** per night, making it one of the most affordable places in town. There's even a shared kitchen if you feel like preparing your own meals, though with so many great restaurants around, you'll probably want to treat yourself to at least a few meals out.

7 EGILSSTAÐIR AND THE EAST FJORDS

7.1 INTRODUCTION TO EGILSSTAÐIR

E gilsstaðir is the central hub when you're exploring the **East Fjords**, and it's where you'll likely find yourself stopping for a bit of calm after the long stretches of driving that this region demands. The town itself sits quietly beside the **Lagarfljót river**, which flows through the valley in wide, slow curves, giving the entire area a peaceful feeling. Unlike the dramatic, towering cliffs you might see elsewhere in the country, here you'll find a gentler landscape, but that doesn't mean it's any less beautiful. The town is surrounded by green hills, and the air always feels fresh, like you're truly far from the rush of daily life.

Egilsstaðir might be small, but it's incredibly practical, and that's why it's the perfect base for you. You've got everything you need right at your fingertips—**grocery stores** like **Bónus** and **Nettó**, **gas stations** if you need to fill up before heading deeper into the fjords, and plenty of **restaurants** and **guesthouses** where you can rest, refuel, and plan your next day. It's not a place where you'll find huge crowds of tourists, even in the height of summer, so you can take your time here, enjoy the calm, and not feel rushed or overwhelmed.

Because of its location, Egilsstaðir makes it really easy for you to explore the surrounding areas. If you're heading south, you can drive towards **Borgarfjörður Eystri**, one of the most stunning yet lesser-known areas of the East Fjords. The fjord is rugged, and you'll often have it almost all to yourself. If you go north, you can head towards **Vopnafjörður**, where the landscape opens up, and you'll get those vast views of the sea meeting the sky.

Egilsstaðir is also the starting point for visiting **Hallormsstaður Forest**, Iceland's largest forest. It's only a short drive away, and once you're there, you can spend hours walking the trails through the trees. It's one of the few places in the country where you can actually lose yourself in a real forest, with tall trees surrounding you and birdsong filling the air. And not too far from the forest is **Hengifoss**, one of Iceland's tallest waterfalls. It's a bit of a hike to reach it, but once you do, the sight of the water plunging down the cliff face, framed by the red layers of the earth, is unforgettable.

In town, you'll notice that things run at a slower pace, and that's part of Egilsstaðir's charm. You won't feel the rush of activity that you get in more tourist-heavy areas, and that gives you a chance to really relax. The town's modern enough that you have everything you need, but it still feels deeply connected to nature, with the river always in the background and the hills just beyond.

If you're visiting during the **winter months**, just keep in mind that some of the roads leading out of Egilsstaðir can be a bit tricky, especially if snow has fallen heavily. The East Fjords are beautiful in winter, but you'll want to check road conditions before heading too far off the main paths. But if you're here in the summer, you'll find that Egilsstaðir gives you the perfect base to explore the rest of this untouched, wild part of the country at your own pace.

7.2 HIKING TO HENGIFOSS WATERFALL

You're going to start the hike to **Hengifoss** by driving along **Route 931** for about **30 minutes** from **Egilsstaðir**. The road will take you alongside **Lagarfljót lake**, and the view will already begin to set the tone for the hike. When you arrive, parking is easy, right near the trailhead. This isn't a long hike—about **2.5 kilometers one way**, so around **5 kilometers total**, but it's uphill almost the whole way. It's not difficult to find your way, and the path is clearly marked, though the incline might feel challenging if you aren't used to hiking, but it's manageable, especially if you take it slow and enjoy the views along the way.

What makes this hike unique is that as soon as you begin, the scenery quickly opens up into a display of **basalt cliffs**, and the landscape around you becomes otherworldly. The basalt columns are layered with **deep red and black rock**, and as you keep going, it feels like you're walking through ancient land, where the earth's history is laid bare right in front of you. These cliffs line the route, and the contrast between the rich colors of the rock and the greenery around you creates a breathtaking visual that makes every step feel worthwhile.

As you continue, you'll come across **Litlanesfoss**, which is a smaller waterfall but no less beautiful, surrounded by tall **basalt columns** that rise like natural sculptures, almost as though they've been crafted by hand, even though they've formed naturally. Take a moment here, enjoy the view, catch your breath, and then get ready to head further up, where the real prize awaits.

Once you reach the top, you'll be standing before **Hengifoss**, which drops from a height of **128 meters**. It's one of the tallest waterfalls you'll find, and the water cascades down over the **red and black basalt layers**, creating a truly dramatic scene that's worth the uphill climb. The colors in the rock, along with the sheer height of the waterfall, make it a sight you won't forget anytime soon.

The best time to hike is during the **summer months**, from **June to September**, when the trail is free from snow and the weather is mild. You can hike it anytime of day, but for the best experience, try going early in the morning or later in the evening when the lighting is softer, and there are fewer people around. The trail is always open, so you have flexibility with timing.

Make sure you're wearing **good hiking boots**, as the trail can be rocky in parts. Bring plenty of **water**, especially since the uphill sections will make you thirsty, and consider packing some **snacks** if you want to take breaks and enjoy the views along the way. It's also smart to carry a **waterproof jacket** since the weather can change quickly, and there's very little shelter along the trail if it rains.

7.3 SEYÐISFJÖRÐUR: THE ART TOWN

When you get to **Seyðisfjörður**, what strikes you immediately is the way the town feels alive with creativity. It's small, but as you walk along the streets, you can't help but notice the **bright, colorful houses** that line the road, each one painted in bold shades that pop against the surrounding mountains. It's a town that feels like it's been painted with a creative touch everywhere you look, but there's nothing over-the-top about it. Everything seems to blend naturally with the stunning fjord and the cascading waterfalls you'll hear in the background as you explore. This place feels special.

One of the first things you'll see is the **Blue Church**, a bright blue building that has become an iconic symbol of the town. It's not just a pretty building to look at—it's also a place where you might stumble upon a live concert, especially during the summer months. And it's right in the heart of the town, so you can't miss it. Just nearby, you've got the **Skaftfell Art Center**, and this is where the town's art scene really comes to life. You're going to want to spend time here, not just passing through. The gallery is always showcasing contemporary work, and it often features artists from all over, making it a great way to get a sense of the creative energy that flows through the town.

Seyðisfjörður is more than just an art hub though. Everywhere you turn, you'll find **art installations** tucked into unexpected places—murals on walls, sculptures outside, and local craft shops where artists display their work. It's the kind of place where the creativity isn't limited to galleries; it's woven into the very fabric of the town, so keep your eyes open as you wander. The whole town feels like an open-air gallery, and you never know when you'll stumble upon something that catches your eye. The vibe here is calm, but it's filled with energy.

The **fjord** that stretches out in front of the town only adds to the atmosphere. Surrounded by **mountains** on all sides, you've got waterfalls crashing down the cliffs in the distance, which creates this stunning natural backdrop that complements the town's creative side. The setting makes everything feel more alive, more vibrant, and it's easy to see why so many artists are drawn here.

In the summer, the town is especially lively, with the **LungA Art Festival** bringing in even more artists, workshops, and performances. But even if you're not visiting during the festival, you'll feel the town's creative spirit in every shop window and art gallery you pass. It's a place that thrives on creativity, and you can feel that in every corner.

7.5 DINING AND ACCOMMODATION IN EGILSSTAÐIR

For a good meal in **Egilsstaðir**, you have to start by heading over to **Salt Café & Bistro** at **Tjarnarbraut 1**. It's easy to find, right in the center of town, and you won't miss it. When you walk in, the atmosphere immediately feels welcoming, and the menu is all about fresh, local ingredients. One of the best things to try here is the **Arctic char**—it's caught locally, and they prepare it in a way that really highlights the flavor. They're open from **11 AM to 9 PM**, so you can stop by for lunch or dinner. Prices are around **3,500 ISK** for a main course, but the food quality and the experience are worth every penny. The restaurant has a casual vibe, and if you're in the mood for a relaxed meal after a long day, this is where you'll want to go.

Another option that's more on the casual side but just as enjoyable is **Askur Pizzeria** on **Egilsstaðavegur 6**. This spot is all about fresh, local ingredients turned into hearty pizzas. They're open from **12 PM to 10 PM**, making it an easy choice for lunch or dinner. A pizza will run you about **2,500 to 3,000 ISK**, which is a good deal considering how much flavor they pack into each one. The place has a relaxed atmosphere, and it's a popular spot with locals, so it's a great way to get a feel for the town. You won't find anything pretentious here, just good food made with care.

For something a bit more upscale, check out the restaurant at **Gisti-húsið - Lake Hotel Egilsstaðir**, which sits on **Egilsstaðavegur**. The hotel dates back to **1903**, and the restaurant has an elegant but still welcoming feel. They focus on dishes made with locally sourced ingredients, so whether you go for the **fresh fish** or the **lamb**, you're going to get something special. The restaurant overlooks **Lagarfljót lake**, so the views while you eat are incredible. They're open from **6 PM to 10 PM**, and while it's more expensive, with main dishes costing around **4,500 ISK**, the food and the setting make it worth the splurge. It's perfect for a quiet, more refined dining experience.

Now, when it comes to where to stay, you can't go wrong with **Lake Hotel Egilsstaðir**. Rooms here start at around **20,000 ISK** per night, and they offer a mix of modern comfort and traditional charm. The hotel is located right by the lake, so you'll have beautiful views right from your window. They also have a spa, which is perfect if you want to relax after a day of exploring. It's a bit on the pricier side, but if you're looking for comfort and a little bit of luxury, this is where you'll want to stay.

If you're traveling on a budget, **Lyngás Guesthouse** at **Lyngási 5** is a great option. It's only about a **10-minute walk** from the center of town, so you're close to everything. Rooms here are simple but clean and comfortable, and prices start at **10,000 ISK** per night. It has a homey feel, and it's a good choice if you're looking for an affordable place to rest while still being in a central location.

For something a little more off the beaten path, consider staying at **Eyjólfsstaðir Guesthouse**, which is just outside of town. It's surrounded by nature, with views of the mountains and countryside that make it a peaceful escape from the hustle and bustle of town. Rooms start at **12,000 ISK** per night, and while it's a simple guesthouse, the surroundings make it feel special. You'll be close enough to town to easily drive in, but far enough out that you can enjoy the tranquility of the Icelandic countryside.

8 AKUREYRI

8.1 INTRODUCTION

Akureyri, the largest town in northern Iceland, feels alive with culture and has this natural beauty that you can't miss. It sits right at the end of **Eyjafjörður**, the longest fjord in the country, and the way the town is tucked between **snow-capped mountains** gives it a calm but vibrant atmosphere at the same time. This town, even though small with around **20,000 people**, feels much bigger because of how much it offers in terms of **arts, history, and local life**.

When you walk around Akureyri, **Hafnarstræti** is where you'll probably find yourself, the main street full of **colorful wooden houses** that date back to the 19th century. These houses, they're not just for looking at—many are still lived in or have been turned into small galleries and shops, giving the whole street this cozy, old-world charm that you won't find in Reykjavik. This street leads you to some of the town's most important cultural spots. You should stop by **Akureyri Art Museum**, located right in the center. It's open from **12 PM to 5 PM**, and at around **1,500 ISK** for entry, it's not going to break the bank. Inside, you'll find an impressive collection of **contemporary art**, a lot of it coming from **local artists**.

Not far from the art museum, down by the waterfront, is the **Hof Cultural and Conference Center**. This is where the town gathers for **concerts, plays, and cultural performances**. The building itself is stunning—sleek, modern, all glass and steel, but it blends so well with the natural surroundings of the fjord and mountains. If you're in Akureyri when there's an event at Hof, you'll definitely want to go. Whether it's a **live music performance** or a **theater show**, the atmosphere inside is electric, with the crowd coming together to enjoy the best that Icelandic culture has to offer. And even if there's nothing on, it's still worth walking around the area to appreciate the architecture and maybe grab a coffee at one of the nearby cafés.

The **Akureyri Church**, designed by **Guðjón Samúelsson**, stands tall over the town on a hill, and you can't miss it. The steps up to the church are steep, but the view at the top is one of the best you'll get in Akureyri. The fjord stretches out below, and the whole town opens up beneath you—it's a great spot to get a sense of the town's layout and its relationship with the surrounding landscape. The church itself, with its clean, modern design, is a symbol of Akureyri, and it's often used for **concerts** or **community events**, so it's much more than just a religious building.

Akureyri also has a thriving **café culture**, and it's one of the best ways to really connect with the local community. Step into **Bláa Kannan Café**, and you'll feel right at home. This place is known not just for its coffee, which is excellent by the way, but also for being a hub where **artists, students, and travelers** mingle. You'll see local artwork hanging on the walls, and the space itself feels warm, with large windows letting in natural light. It's easy to lose a few hours here, just sitting with a coffee and watching the world go by. The town's cafés are like mini-galleries themselves, often displaying the works of **local artists**, so you get this creative vibe wherever you go.

Another thing that sets Akureyri apart is its connection to **education and innovation** through the **University of Akureyri**. The presence of the university brings a youthful, intellectual energy to the town. You'll notice students around town, especially in the parks or the cafés, giving the place a fresh, modern feel despite its historic charm. The university also hosts talks, workshops, and cultural events, which adds even more to the town's vibrant cultural life.

Akureyri's **festivals** are another highlight. Every year, the **Akureyri Winter Festival** transforms the town into a hub for winter sports and outdoor events. Picture this: outdoor concerts, ice skating, and skiing competitions. It feels like the whole town comes together to celebrate winter. If you're here in the summer, the **Akureyri Art Festival** is something to look out for. The streets are filled with performances, exhibitions, and **interactive art installations**, giving you a sense of how deeply rooted art and creativity are in this town.

The town's unique **architecture** also stands out. While the colorful wooden houses give Akureyri its traditional look, the **modern buildings** like the Hof Cultural Center and Akureyri Church show that this is a town looking toward the future. It's this mix of old and new that makes the town so special. As you walk around, you'll notice **public art installations, sculptures, and murals**. The town feels like an open-air gallery, where every corner reveals something new, whether it's a piece of art or a stunning view of the fjord.

8.2 TOP ATTRACTIONS

At the **Botanical Gardens**, the first thing you'll notice is how peaceful it feels. This spot, located on **Eyrarlandsvegur,** is one of the best places to escape the buzz of the town and just relax. What's unique here is the sheer variety of plants—**7,000 species**, with a special focus on the hardy Icelandic flora that thrives despite the tough climate. The garden is open from **8 AM to 10 PM** during summer, and you don't have to worry about any entrance fees. It's perfect for a slow stroll, and if you've got time, head into the **greenhouses**, where you'll find tropical plants flourishing in this northern environment. Every path leads to a new pocket of greenery, and it's easy to lose track of time here, surrounded by the scent of flowers and the soft rustle of leaves in the breeze.

Next, make your way to the **Old Town** along **Hafnarstræti** and **Aðalstræti**, where the colorful **19th-century wooden houses** have a charm that's hard to resist. Walking through this part of town feels like you've stepped back in time, with narrow streets and well-preserved buildings that have witnessed the town's history unfold. Each house tells a story, and it's not just about the architecture—it's about the **craftsmanship** that went into making these homes, many of which are still lived in today. While you're here, take the time to explore some of the **local artisan shops**, where you can find handmade crafts that are perfect for souvenirs. The **Akureyri Museum** is also located on **Aðalstræti 58**—you can't miss it. Open from **10 AM to 5 PM**, it's an easy stop where for about **1,500 ISK**, you get a look into the past, learning about everything from **fishing and farming** to **Viking history**. This museum isn't overwhelming, but it's packed with interesting details about how the locals have lived through the centuries, surviving and thriving in this northern corner of the world.

Climbing up the steps to the **Akureyri Church** on **Eyrarlandsvegur** is worth the effort for the view alone. This church, designed by **Guðjón Samúelsson**, looks simple from the outside, but its twin spires dominate the skyline. Inside, you'll find a beautiful **stained glass window** that tells stories of Iceland's Christian past, and if you're lucky, you might even catch a **concert** there—something that happens quite often. The best part, though, is the view from the top of the steps. You get this wide, panoramic look over the town, the fjord, and the surrounding mountains, which is something you can't quite experience anywhere else in town. The church is open from **9 AM to 6 PM**, and it's free to enter, making it a no-brainer to visit whether you're interested in architecture or just want to see the best view around.

If you love art, you'll want to stop by the **Akureyri Art Museum** on **Kaupvangsstræti**. It's a small museum, but it's the heart of the contemporary art scene here in northern Iceland. Open from **12 PM to 5 PM** with an entry fee of **1,500 ISK**, the museum offers a rotating set of exhibitions featuring both **local and international artists**. You never know what you'll find, but the variety ensures there's always something engaging to see. Whether it's a thought-provoking installation or a colorful painting that captures the wildness of the Icelandic landscape, it's a great spot to spend an afternoon if you're in the mood for something more creative.

For something more historical, visit the **Nonni House** on **Aðalstræti**, one of the oldest buildings in the town, built in **1850**. The house has been turned into a small museum dedicated to **Jón Sveinsson**, also known as Nonni, who was a famous Icelandic author of children's books. Open from **11 AM to 5 PM** with an entry fee of **500 ISK**, it gives you a peek into how life was lived in Akureyri over a century ago. The rooms are small and simple, with period furniture and a cozy atmosphere that makes you feel like you've stepped into the past. It's a quick stop but worth it, especially if you're interested in literature or Iceland's cultural history.

If you're visiting during the winter months, make sure to head up to **Hlíðarfjall Ski Resort**, which is just a **10-minute drive** from town. It's the main ski area in northern Iceland, and you'll find plenty of slopes whether you're a beginner or a more experienced skier. The resort is open from **10 AM to 4 PM**, and a full-day pass costs around **4,000 ISK**, which is pretty reasonable. In the summer, this area transforms into a hiker's paradise, with trails that offer stunning views over the town and fjord. No matter the season, the surrounding mountains are breathtaking, and spending a few hours up here is an excellent way to get in touch with the natural beauty of the area.

For some relaxation, head over to the **Akureyri Swimming Pool** on **Þingvallastræti**. It's a favorite among locals, and for good reason. The pools are heated, so it doesn't matter what the weather is like—you'll be nice and warm. There are also **hot tubs, saunas**, and even a

waterslide, making it a fun stop whether you're looking to unwind or have some fun. Open from **6:45 AM to 9 PM** on weekdays and shorter hours on weekends, it's a place where you can soak in the water and just relax while taking in the surrounding views of the mountains. Entry costs around **1,000 ISK**, and it's well worth it for the experience.

All these spots are close enough together that you can explore them easily on foot, and each one offers a glimpse into the town's history, culture, or natural beauty. There's so much to see and do here that you'll never run out of things to visit.

8.3 VISITING THE SURROUNDING AREA

You'll want to start your day by heading straight to **Goðafoss**. It's just a **45-minute drive** from Akureyri along **Route 1**—an easy road to follow, and the moment you see the signs, you'll know you're close. Now, what's special about Goðafoss isn't just the name, which translates to the "Waterfall of the Gods," but the sheer beauty and power of it. You'll hear the roar of the water long before you catch sight of the wide, majestic horseshoe-shaped falls. There's no entry fee, and while you can visit at any time of day, it's always best to go in the morning or early afternoon if you want to have a quieter experience. The pathways around the waterfall allow you to get close enough to feel the mist on your face, so be sure to watch your step—the rocks can be slippery, and the spray from the water is constant. Take your time, plan to stay for at least **45 minutes to an hour**, and don't rush. You'll want to walk along both sides of the river to get different angles of the falls. Each side gives you a unique perspective, whether you're gazing at the waterfall from a distance or standing right up close.

When you're ready to move on, the next stop should be **Lake Mývatn**, which is about **another hour's drive east** on **Route 1**. This area is a hub for volcanic activity, with craters, hot springs, and unique rock formations all around the lake. There's no entrance fee to explore the lake, but specific attractions, like the **Mývatn Nature Baths**, do charge. If you're in the mood for some relaxation, the **Nature Baths**, located at **Jarðbaðshólar**, are open from **12 PM to 10 PM**, and entry costs around **5,500 ISK**. These geothermal baths are the perfect way to unwind after a morning of sightseeing. The water is a soft blue, heated naturally by the earth, and unlike some of the more tourist-heavy spots in the south, you'll find the atmosphere here much more peaceful and laid-back. Bring your swimsuit and towel, and plan to spend a couple of hours here, soaking in the warmth and letting your mind wander while you gaze out at the surrounding mountains and volcanic fields.

Once you've recharged, hop back in the car and drive just a few minutes to **Hverir**, which sits close to **Krafla**. This is where things start to look otherworldly. The geothermal area here is filled with **bubbling mud pots** and **steaming fumaroles** that rise up from the colorful earth. The smell of sulfur hits you immediately, and the ground beneath your feet is alive with heat and energy. Visiting **Hverir** is free, and since it's open at all times, you can explore at your leisure, but I recommend going early or late in the day to avoid the crowds. The landscape is truly alien—reds, yellows, and browns stretch out before you, and steam rises from cracks in the earth. The paths are well marked, and it's essential you stay on them because the ground can be unstable in places. You'll only need about **30 to 45 minutes** to see everything, but the experience will stay with you long after you've left.

Next, you'll want to head to **Dettifoss**, the most powerful waterfall in Europe, located in **Vatnajökull National Park**. It's a bit of a drive, about **1.5 to 2 hours** from Lake Mývatn, but once you arrive, you'll understand why it's worth the trip. You can approach the falls from either **Route 862** or **Route 864**, but **Route 862** offers a better-maintained road and access to a viewing platform that's easier to navigate. There's no fee to visit Dettifoss, and the waterfall is open all year, though if you're traveling in winter, be prepared for some snow and ice along the roads. You'll want to spend at least **an hour** here, taking in the power and force of the water as it crashes into the canyon below. You can hear Dettifoss from a distance, but nothing prepares you for the sight up close. It's loud, it's intense, and the spray will likely get you wet, so a rain jacket is a good idea. Dettifoss is more than just a stop—it's an experience of nature at its most raw and untamed.

On your way back, there's a quick stop you should make at **Grjó-tagjá**, a small lava cave that holds a hot spring inside. It's just a short drive from **Lake Mývatn**, and while you can no longer bathe in the water, it's still a stunning sight to see. The water is a deep blue, and the cave itself feels hidden and quiet, making it the perfect spot for a short visit. You only need about **15 minutes** here, but it's well worth it for the unique atmosphere and chance to see something that feels secret and off the beaten path.

If you still have energy, **Aldeyjarfoss** is another incredible water-fall that fewer people know about. It's a bit more of a trek, located about **1.5 hours** from Akureyri, and you'll need to drive along a gravel road off **Route 842** to get there. But once you arrive, you'll see the waterfall framed by towering **basalt columns**, creating a dramatic and photogenic scene. There's no fee to visit, and it's accessible year-round, but winter can make the roads tricky. You'll want to stay for about **45 minutes to an hour**, wandering around the falls and taking in the peaceful beauty of the area. The best time to go is in the early morning or late afternoon when the light is soft, and the crowds are minimal.

Good to know: These day trips from Akureyri offer a great mix of natural experiences, all easily reachable by car.

8.4 WINTER ACTIVITIES

If you plan to spend the winter in this part of northern Iceland, there's no better place to start than **Hlíðarfjall**, the ski resort that's only a quick drive away from town—just about **5 kilometers** heading west along **Route 821**. The resort itself opens its lifts at **10 AM**, so I'd recommend getting there early to avoid the midday rush. Now, whether you've never skied before or you're a seasoned expert, there's a slope for you. The trails are well-maintained, and you can rent all your gear right on-site if you didn't bring your own. And **lift tickets**? They'll set you back around **5,000 ISK** for a full day, which is well worth it because you'll want to soak in the views from the top of the runs—the fjord spreads out below you, and on clear days, the blue skies make the snow-covered peaks almost sparkle. If you're in for something a little different, there are even **night skiing sessions** on certain evenings, where they light up the slopes so you can ski under the stars. The cold feels different up here, sharp but invigorating, especially when you're skiing or snowboarding with the fjord below. **Make sure you're dressed warmly**, though; it gets colder as the day moves on.

If skiing isn't your thing or you're just looking for another kind of thrill, **snowmobiling** is a perfect way to experience the raw winter landscapes. You can book a tour with **IceAk**, which is easy to find in the heart of town, right on **Hafnarstræti**. From there, you'll head up into the mountains where the snow stretches as far as the eye can see. The tours last around **1-2 hours**, and for about **25,000 ISK**, you'll get an unforgettable experience of zooming across untouched snow, seeing the northern fjords from a totally different perspective. The company provides all the safety gear you'll need—helmets, gloves, and full-body overalls—so you won't have to worry about staying warm. Just make sure to hold on tight because those snowmobiles move fast, and the views are absolutely incredible the whole way.

Book ahead of time, though, because these tours fill up fast, especially when the weather is clear.

Then, of course, there's the big draw that brings so many people here during the long winter nights—the **Northern Lights**. If the sky is clear, you don't even need to go far. You can step just outside the town center to **Krossanesborgir**, a nature reserve just a **10-minute drive north** along **Route 821**. The best part? It's completely free, and because it's away from the town's lights, the darkness makes for an ideal setting to catch the auroras. If you want something a little more structured, though, there are plenty of **Northern Lights tours** offered locally. These tours usually run between **October and March**, costing around **8,000 ISK** per person, and they'll take you to the best spots for aurora viewing, well away from any light pollution. It's all about timing and patience, so **check the aurora forecast** before heading out, and dress warmly because you could be waiting out there for a while. But when the sky lights up with green and purple waves of light, it's worth every moment.

After a day filled with outdoor activities or long nights chasing the Northern Lights, there's no better way to unwind than soaking in one of Iceland's famous geothermal pools. Right in the town center, you'll find the **Akureyri Swimming Pool** on **Þingvallastræti**. Open year-round from **6:45 AM to 9 PM** during the week, with later hours on weekends, it costs about **1,000 ISK** to enter. The water is naturally heated, and when you're sitting in the warm pools surrounded by the cold winter air, it's an unbeatable way to relax. The pool is incredibly popular with locals, and you'll find that the atmosphere is relaxed and friendly, making it a great spot to not only soak but also get a sense of daily life in northern Iceland.

If you prefer something a bit quieter but still active, **snowshoeing** is the way to go. You can rent snowshoes right in town, and then head to **Kjarnaskógur Forest**, which is just a short **10-minute drive south** along **Route 821**. It's a beautiful, peaceful place to walk through, especially in winter when the trees are heavy with snow and the paths are nearly silent except for the crunching sound of your shoes. There's no entrance fee, and the forest is open all day, though you'll want to go during daylight hours for the best experience. It's the perfect way to enjoy the quiet solitude of Icelandic nature without the rush or crowds of busier winter sports.

Finally, for a good winter experience, there's **dog sledding**. **Akureyri Dog Sledding** offers tours that take you out into the snowy plains with a team of sled dogs pulling you along. These tours typically last about half a day, with prices starting around **20,000 ISK** per person. The dogs are enthusiastic and well-trained, and you'll get the chance to ride through snow-covered fields with nothing but the sound of the sled cutting through the snow and the occasional bark from the dogs. It's an exhilarating and special way to explore the landscape, and the tour guides will make sure you're comfortable and safe, even if it's your first time trying dog sledding.

8.5 WHERE TO STAY AND EAT

When you're hungry and looking for somewhere memorable to eat, start by heading straight to **Strikið**, which is easy to find on **Skipagata 14**. It's got one of the best spots in town, right on the rooftop, where you can take in views of the fjord while you eat. **The food here is special,** focused on fresh Icelandic ingredients, particularly fish and lamb, both of which are locally sourced and cooked with great care. You should plan to spend around **5,000-7,000 ISK** for a meal, but it's worth every bit when you taste dishes like their **grilled lamb fillet**— tender, full of flavor, and served with vegetables that are perfectly seasoned. They're open from **11:30 AM to 10 PM**, so you've got plenty of time to stop by for lunch or dinner. The place is known for its sophisticated atmosphere, but it's not stuffy, and the staff are always friendly and helpful if you need recommendations.

For something a bit more relaxed but still with great food, you want to visit **Blaa Kannan Café**. It's on **Hafnarstræti 96**, and you really can't miss the bright blue building—just seeing it makes you want to step inside. This café is all about comfort, with a warm, inviting interior that makes it perfect for a lazy morning or a quiet afternoon. The prices here are easier on your wallet, with most meals costing between **1,500 and 3,000 ISK**. They're open from **9 AM to 6 PM**, and one thing you have to try is their **carrot cake**—it's incredibly moist and the perfect companion to a cup of coffee. The menu is simple, focusing on soups, sandwiches, and light meals, but everything is made fresh, and you can taste the quality in every bite. It's a great place to sit and relax, especially if you're looking to take a break from walking around town.

Now, if seafood is what you're after, then you'll want to check out **Rub23**, located on **Kaupvangsstræti 6**. This place is a fusion of Icelandic seafood and Asian-inspired flavors, so if you're craving something a bit different, you'll love it. The sushi here is a standout, especially if you're in the mood for something fresh and light, and their **pan-fried Arctic char** is another must-try. It's a bit pricier, with meals running around **6,000-8,000 ISK**, but the food is consistently excellent. They're open from **5 PM to 11 PM**, so it's more of a dinner spot, and you'll definitely want to reserve a table, especially on the weekends when it gets busy. The mix of flavors here, with Icelandic fish paired with Asian sauces and spices, really sets it apart from other restaurants in the area.

If you're after something hearty and casual, **Greifinn** on **Glerárgata 20** is the way to go. It's a local favorite and perfect if you want a big, filling meal without any fuss. Prices here range from **2,500 to 4,000 ISK**, so it's a bit more budget-friendly, and they're known for serving classic Icelandic comfort food like **lamb soup** and **fish and chips**. They're open from **11:30 AM to 10 PM**, and the portions are generous, which makes it a great choice if you're really hungry after a day of sightseeing. The atmosphere here is laid-back, and it's the kind of place you can bring friends or family for a relaxed meal.

For a good night's sleep, you have a few excellent options. If you're looking for something upscale, **Hotel Kea** on **Hafnarstræti 87-89** is a great choice. This hotel has been around since **1944**, so it's got a lot of history, and the rooms are comfortable and classic. You'll be right in the heart of town, close to everything, and the rooms start at around **20,000 ISK** per night. They also serve a nice breakfast buffet, so you can fuel up before heading out to explore the area. The hotel itself is a bit of a landmark, and the service is excellent—just what you need after a long day of travel.

If you're after something more affordable, **Guesthouse Akureyri** on **Hafnarstræti 108** is a cozy and comfortable option. Rooms here are around **10,000 ISK** per night, and while it's a simpler place, it's still very comfortable, and the location couldn't be better. You'll be within walking distance of everything in town, so you won't need to worry about getting around. The rooms are clean, many with great views of the surrounding mountains, and the atmosphere is laid-back and welcoming, making it a great choice if you're looking for somewhere low-key but still charming.

For a more modern stay, try **Icelandair Hotel Akureyri** on **Þingvallastræti 23**. This place is sleek and stylish, with rooms starting at around **18,000 ISK** per night. The hotel is just a short walk from the **Botanical Gardens**, and it has its own restaurant that focuses on seasonal, local ingredients, so you don't have to go far for a good meal. The rooms are modern and comfortable, and the staff can help you book tours or give recommendations on what to see and do while you're in town. It's a great option if you like a hotel with a more contemporary feel but still want a connection to the local culture.

No matter what you're looking for, whether it's a cozy café, a hearty meal, or a comfortable place to rest, you'll find plenty of choices that will make your stay memorable. Trust me!

9 ÍSAFJÖRÐUR AND THE WILD WESTFJORDS

9.1 ÍSAFJÖRÐUR

When you step into **this remote town**, you'll instantly feel how deeply connected it is to the land and sea around it. The mountains aren't just a backdrop—they almost feel like they're part of the town itself, towering above and giving the whole area a rugged, raw beauty. You're going to see old houses, most of them made from wood and painted in bright colors—these are reminders of the fishing village this place used to be, and even though the pace has slowed, **fishing is still very much part of life here**. The harbor is small but active, and the boats you see are still heading out to sea, bringing in fresh catch that ends up on your plate in one of the local restaurants.

Life here moves slowly, but that's part of what makes it special. It's not a busy place, and you won't find a lot of crowds or noise. Instead, you get this deep sense of peace that's hard to find anywhere else. You'll notice that people take their time, and when you walk through the narrow streets, you'll feel like you've stepped back in time

—yet it doesn't feel stuck in the past. You'll hear about small festivals, maybe even stumble upon one, where the community comes together to celebrate with local music, art, and food. **Summers here are filled with light**, and the long days stretch out, giving you plenty of time to explore, but it's the sense of space and quiet that will stay with you.

In the winter, the town takes on a different kind of beauty. Everything slows down even more. The snow comes down heavy, and the streets and houses look like something out of a picture book, blanketed in white. People here are used to the long, dark days, and you'll see how they adapt, making the most of the coziness that comes with the cold months. This is when you might catch the **Northern Lights** dancing across the sky, a sight that's hard to describe but one you won't forget.

You're going to find that this place isn't just about the landscape—it's also about the people and the stories they carry. **Fishing runs deep here**, and it's something you'll hear about when you talk to locals. The sea has shaped everything, from the buildings to the way people live, and you'll feel that in every corner of the town. But beyond that, there's a strong sense of creativity here. You'll find **art galleries, small studios, and music events** that might surprise you for such a small place. The town has become something of an arts hub in the Westfjords, and that mix of traditional fishing life and modern creativity gives it a really unique energy.

When you're walking along the waterfront or sitting at a café looking out over the fjord, you'll see fishing boats in the distance, framed by the **mountains that rise steeply from the water**, and it will hit you how isolated but beautiful this place is. **The weather changes fast** here, so one minute, you might have clear views across the fjord, and the next, mist rolls in, covering everything in a soft, quiet fog. But that's all part of the charm—this place forces you to slow down and take things as they come.

This town is far from the busier, more tourist-heavy areas, and that's exactly why you'll want to come here. It's a place where you can **disconnect from everything** and just be surrounded by nature. And though you might be far from big cities, you'll never feel too far from the warmth of the community, the local traditions, and the rhythm of life that's deeply tied to the land and sea around you.

9.2 DYNJANDI WATERFALL

Dynjandi is **not just any waterfall**—it's the crown jewel of the West-fjords, and as soon as you get close, you'll understand why. It cascades down a cliffside in layers, like a massive, wide bridal veil, dropping over 100 meters in total. The water spreads out as it falls, which gives it that distinctive fan shape, making it one of the most photogenic spots in the area. When you're standing at the base of Dynjandi, the sound of the water crashing down is almost deafening, and you'll feel the mist on your face long before you reach the main falls. The whole scene is **raw, powerful, and completely mesmerizing**.

To get to Dynjandi, **you'll drive along Route 60**, which winds through the beautiful but rugged landscape of the Westfjords. If you're coming from Ísafjörður, it's about an hour and a half by car, and the drive itself is worth the trip, with breathtaking views of the fjords and mountains along the way. The road is part gravel, so **take it slow**, especially if the weather turns. Once you reach the parking area, which is free, it's a fairly easy hike to the waterfall. You'll walk up a rocky path for about 15 to 20 minutes, passing by a series of smaller waterfalls like Hundafoss and Bæjarfoss. Each of these smaller falls has its own charm, but **they're just the warm-up** for the grand spectacle that awaits you at the top.

When you finally arrive at the base of Dynjandi, **you'll be struck by the sheer scale of it**. The water starts narrow at the top, but by the time it reaches the bottom, it's spread out to over 30 meters wide. The sound, the sight, and the feel of the place will grab you immediately. It's one of those places where you'll want to spend a good amount of time, just standing there and letting it all sink in. **You can get really close to the waterfall**, right up to where the water hits the rocks, but be careful—the spray makes the rocks slippery, so be sure you've got good shoes on.

The best time to visit Dynjandi is during the summer months when the weather is more predictable, and the midnight sun means you've got long hours of daylight to enjoy. **You can visit at any time of day**, and since there's no entry fee or official closing time, it's up to you how long you want to stay. If you come late in the evening, you might find you have the place almost to yourself, which makes it even more magical. In winter, though, **the road can be impassable due to snow**, so always check the conditions before heading out. The Westfjords can be tricky to navigate in winter, and Dynjandi isn't the easiest place to reach if the weather turns.

There's a lot of history tied to Dynjandi as well. It's been a landmark for sailors navigating the fjords for centuries, and its name, which means "thundering," perfectly describes the sound you'll hear as you approach. The waterfall has long been a source of fascination and pride for the locals, and once you've stood in front of it, you'll see why. It's not just the size of it—it's the way it fits into the landscape. The mountains, the valley, and the fjord all come together to create a setting that feels almost otherworldly. You won't find any shops or restaurants nearby, so **be sure to bring water, snacks, and anything else you might need**. It's a remote spot, and part of its appeal is the sense that you're standing in a place that hasn't changed much in centuries.

After you've spent time at the falls, there are trails that lead further into the surrounding area. If you're up for more hiking, you can explore these paths and discover some quieter spots away from the main trail. The view from the top of Dynjandi, looking out over the fjord below, is worth the effort, and it's one of those moments where you'll be glad you made the trip all the way out here. It's a place that stays with you long after you've left, **a true highlight of any visit to the Westfjords**.

9.3 RAUÐASANDUR BEACH

Rauðasandur Beach is truly special because it stands out from almost every other beach you might visit in Iceland, and even beyond. What makes it different, and immediately catches your eye, is the **unique**

reddish sand that seems to change color depending on the light and the time of day. At some points, it looks golden, then it shifts to pink or even deep shades of copper and red. The beach stretches for nearly **10 kilometers**, and its remote location means you often have the chance to experience it in complete solitude, which is a rare gift in a country as popular with tourists as Iceland. You can **walk for miles and feel like you're the only person in the world**, with nothing around you except the endless red sand, the sound of the waves, and the soft wind.

Getting to Rauðasandur is part of the adventure. You'll be driving along **Route 612**, a gravel road that winds through some of the most dramatic landscapes of the Westfjords. The drive takes around **45 minutes from Patreksfjörður**, and while the road isn't paved, it's manageable if you take it slow, especially if you're not used to gravel roads. The final descent down toward the beach is steep and narrow, but **once you reach the valley**, the views of the beach spreading out in front of you are absolutely worth the effort. There's no entrance fee, and **the beach is open all the time**, so you're free to come whenever you want, but most people recommend visiting during **low tide**, when you can walk further out onto the sand and experience just how vast and empty it feels.

One of the first things you'll notice when you step onto Rauðasandur is the sheer **quiet**. There are no shops, no facilities, no crowds—just you and the landscape. It's important to **come prepared**, as there's nowhere to buy food or water, so bring everything you need for the day, including snacks, water, and warm layers. The wind can pick up quickly, and the weather changes fast in this part of the country, so you'll want to dress in layers to stay comfortable.

The best way to experience Rauðasandur is simply to **walk along the beach**, taking in the colors of the sand and watching the waves. If you're lucky, you might spot **seals** basking on the shore or playing in the water, but remember to give them space. There's also plenty of opportunities for **birdwatching** here, with puffins and other seabirds often making their nests in the cliffs around the beach. If you're into photography, this place is an absolute dream—the contrasts between the sand, the sea, and the sky create stunning visuals, especially in the evening when the light becomes softer and the beach takes on a golden glow.

For those who enjoy a bit more activity, there are several hiking trails around Rauðasandur. **You can hike up into the surrounding hills**, which will give you a panoramic view of the beach and the fjords beyond. The hikes aren't difficult, but they're steep, so take your time and enjoy the journey. Once you reach the top, you'll be rewarded with one of the most breathtaking views in all of Iceland.

Historically, Rauðasandur has long been a place of solitude and mystery. Legends say that outlaws once hid in the mountains above the beach, and you can almost feel that sense of isolation and escape when you're there. **This is a place that hasn't changed much in centuries**, and you'll feel that connection to the past as you walk along the shore.

The best time to visit is during the summer months, when **the road is accessible**, and the weather is more predictable. In winter, **the road can become impassable due to snow**, so it's best to plan your visit between June and September. Even in summer, be sure to check the road conditions before you go, as the weather in the Westfjords can be unpredictable.

Rauðasandur is not the kind of place where you'll find tourist crowds or bustling activity. **It's a quiet escape, a place to reconnect with nature and experience the raw, untouched beauty of Iceland**. Whether you're coming for a few hours or spending the whole day there, you'll leave with a sense of peace and wonder that's hard to find anywhere else.

CHAPTER 9

9.4 PUFFIN WATCHING AT LÁTRABJARG CLIFFS

This spot is all about the birds, especially puffins, which you'll see up close—sometimes so close you can almost reach out and touch them, but resist the temptation to disturb them. **What makes this place so incredible isn't just the puffins** though, it's the sheer size of the cliffs. Stretching out for 14 kilometers and towering as high as 400 meters above the Atlantic Ocean, it's something you just have to see in person to really grasp.

The drive to Látrabjarg feels like a true adventure. You'll be coming along **Route 612**, and it's not a quick trip—expect to spend about **1.5 hours driving from Patreksfjörður**. The road itself is gravel, not paved, so take your time. There are some steep areas, and you want to make sure you're driving safely. This is the kind of place where you really feel like you're traveling off the beaten path. Once you arrive, you'll find a small parking area. From there, it's just a short walk to the cliffs where the puffins nest.

You don't need to worry about opening times or fees because **Látrabjarg is open all the time**, and there's no charge to visit. However, to see the puffins, the best time to come is between **May and August**, with **late June to early July** being peak puffin season. If you come during the day, the puffins might be out fishing at sea, so aim to visit in the late afternoon or evening when they're returning to their nests. This way, you'll see hundreds of them flying back to their burrows along the cliffs, carrying food to their chicks.

Now, one thing you've got to be careful about is sticking to the marked paths. The puffins dig burrows close to the cliff's edge, and if you step off the path, you could damage their nests without realizing it. Also, the ground near the edge can be a bit unstable, and the drop is extreme. You'll want to keep a safe distance from the cliffside, especially since the winds can be strong here, and the ocean far below is no joke.

As you walk along the cliff, you'll notice it's not just puffins. **You'll also see razorbills, guillemots, fulmars**, and many other seabirds making their nests in the cliffs. This place is one of the most important bird cliffs in the world, and it's truly something special to witness all this life clinging to the steep rock faces. **Bring a good camera**, because you're going to want to capture these moments, especially if you're there around sunset when the light softens and the whole cliff starts glowing.

A bit of history to keep in mind while you're there—this area used to be known for dramatic rescues. **In the past, locals risked their lives to climb down these cliffs to rescue sailors** whose ships had wrecked in the waters below. It's a reminder of just how rugged and dangerous this part of the world can be, where the cliffs meet the open ocean and life depends on a deep connection to the land and sea.

As for what to bring, **make sure you're dressed for the weather**. Even if it looks sunny, the wind here can be harsh, and the temperature can drop quickly. A good windproof jacket and sturdy shoes are essential, especially since you'll be walking on uneven ground near the edge of some pretty high cliffs. If you're planning on staying a while, it's smart to bring snacks and water with you. There are no facilities here—no shops, no cafes, just you and the wild cliffs.

Visiting **Látrabjarg Cliffs is really about the experience of being in nature**—you're far from the crowds and the tourist centers, and that sense of isolation adds to the magic. The quiet here is only broken by the sound of the wind and the seabirds. It's one of those places where you feel like time slows down, and the raw beauty of the landscape takes over.

The best time to visit is during the summer months, but always check the weather and road conditions before you set out. Even in summer, **the roads can be tricky after heavy rain** or if the weather's been unpredictable, so it's always better to be prepared.

9.5 DINING AND ACCOMMODATION IN THE WESTFJORDS

When you're in Ísafjörður, **Tjöruhúsið** is more than just a meal—it's the kind of place that gives you a real sense of the town's deep connection to the sea. You walk into this old wooden building, nestled right by the harbor, and immediately you know you're in for something special. **They cook everything fresh;** fish straight from the ocean—cod, halibut, and the Icelandic staple, wolffish. The price for the buffet is around **6,500 ISK**, and you can keep going back for more, so don't hold back. It's open from **12 p.m. to 10 p.m.**, and the earlier you arrive, the better because this place fills up fast. **No reservations for lunch**, just walk in and take your chances—trust me, it's worth it.

Now, if you're looking for something a little more relaxed, head over to **Húsið** on **Aðalstræti**, just a short stroll from the harbor. It's a laid-back café where locals come for coffee and a bite, and it's the perfect spot to settle in after a day of exploring. **Meals here are simple but hearty**—you'll find Icelandic lamb soup, burgers, and more, all priced between **3,000 and 5,000 ISK**. You can come in any time between **11 a.m. and 10 p.m.**, so whether you want to grab a quick lunch or sit down for a relaxed dinner, it's a great choice. The atmosphere is cozy, the service warm, and you'll feel right at home, no matter how long you stay.

For your stay in Ísafjörður, **Guesthouse Ísafjörður** is a solid option if you want something simple, clean, and close to everything. Located near the harbor, this place offers **basic rooms priced around 15,000 to 25,000 ISK per night**, depending on the time of year. **Breakfast is usually included**, and it's the kind of spread that sets you up perfectly for a day of exploring—fresh local bread, skyr (a thick Icelandic yogurt), and plenty of coffee. It's nothing fancy, but the comfort and location make it a great base. Plus, it's easy to get around from here, with everything just a few minutes' walk away.

If you're after something with a bit more comfort and a touch of luxury, **Hotel Ísafjörður** on **Silfurtorg Square** is the place to be. It's a modern hotel with rooms offering stunning views over the fjord, perfect for unwinding after a day spent out in the wild beauty of the Westfjords. Prices range between **20,000 and 35,000 ISK per night**, and the in-house restaurant specializes in **local cuisine**, serving dishes like **lamb fillet or Arctic char**. Dinner here will cost you anywhere between **4,000 and 8,000 ISK**, depending on what you order, and you'll be treated to some of the finest local ingredients, carefully prepared and presented. **It's modern comfort with an authentic Icelandic touch**, giving you the best of both worlds.

But if you really want to get away from it all, consider staying at **Heydalur Guesthouse**, which is about **100 kilometers away in Mjóifjörður Valley**. You're truly out in the wilderness here, surrounded by mountains, and the guesthouse itself is run by a welcoming family that makes you feel like you've been invited into their home. **There's a geothermal hot pool right outside**, and trust me, you won't want to miss soaking in those warm waters after a long day exploring the fjords. Rooms here range from **12,000 to 22,000 ISK per night**, and they serve up meals made with fresh local ingredients, with **Arctic char** being a highlight on the menu. Prices for meals are around **3,500 to 6,500 ISK**, and everything here is made with care, creating an intimate, personal experience. Staying here is about feeling like you've been let in on a secret—**a hidden gem of a place where nature and comfort meet**.

10 PRACTICAL INFORMATION FOR TRAVELING

10.1 TRANSPORTATION

When you will arrive in Iceland, you'll quickly realize that **traffic** is generally light and easy to manage, especially once you get out of Reykjavík. In the city, you might hit a bit of traffic during peak hours, but nothing like the gridlock you'd expect in major metropolitan areas. On the **Ring Road** (Route 1), which circles the country, traffic is sparse, and driving is straightforward, making it ideal for those who enjoy scenic drives with very few interruptions. The thing to remember, though, is that weather can change quickly, and roads can become icy or snowy, especially in the winter months, so always check **road.is** for real-time updates and conditions.

Renting a car is, without a doubt, the most flexible and convenient way to get around Iceland, especially for tourists who want the freedom to explore the country's stunning landscapes at their own pace. The **Ring Road** connects most of the main attractions and towns, but to reach those off-the-beaten-path spots like hidden waterfalls or remote hot springs, a car is essential. Rental prices vary, but expect to pay around €40-€100 per day depending on the season and type of vehicle. In the summer, a standard car will do the job, but if you're venturing into the highlands or driving in winter, you'll want to go for a **4x4**, which can handle rougher terrain and unpredictable weather.

Most tourists prefer renting a car because it allows them to take spontaneous stops at breathtaking views or spend more time at places like **Jökulsárlón Glacier Lagoon** or the **Golden Circle** without being tied to a tour schedule. You can find rental car agencies at **Keflavík International Airport, Reykjavík**, and other major towns. Be sure to book in advance, especially in peak tourist seasons like summer and Christmas.

If you're not comfortable driving, or simply prefer public transportation, **buses** are a good option for getting between towns. The **Strætó** bus system serves Reykjavík and some nearby areas, with ticket prices ranging from €3-€4 for a single ride. For long-distance routes, buses run to larger towns like **Akureyri** and **Selfoss**, but keep in mind that service can be limited in more remote areas, especially during winter. A one-way bus ticket from **Reykjavík** to **Akureyri** is around €55, and the journey takes about 6 hours. You can purchase tickets online or at the bus terminals, but buses are not always the most convenient option if you want to visit more isolated attractions.

Another thing to consider is **domestic flights**, which are especially popular during winter when road conditions can be tricky. **Icelandair** and **Air Iceland Connect** operate regular flights between **Reykjavík Domestic Airport** and places like **Akureyri** and **Egilsstaðir**. Flights are quick, often under an hour, and prices vary, but you can expect to pay between €50-€150 depending on the season and booking time. This can be a good option if you're planning to skip long drives and want to avoid the unpredictable road conditions during the colder months.

For those who don't want to drive or take buses, **guided tours** offer a convenient way to see the country. These tours, which range from half-day trips to multi-day adventures, cover major sights like the **Golden Circle**, **South Coast**, and **Snæfellsnes Peninsula**, and can be tailored to include activities like glacier hiking or whale watching. Prices for these tours can range from €80 for a basic half-day tour to **€300 or more** for multi-day tours with accommodations included. While guided tours are a more structured way to travel, they take the hassle out of planning and navigating, especially if you're unfamiliar with the area or uncomfortable driving in Iceland's weather.

In terms of **convenience**, most tourists prefer **car rentals** for the freedom and flexibility they offer, allowing them to venture off the main roads and explore Iceland's hidden gems. However, if you're not confident driving in a foreign country, especially in winter, **buses** and **domestic flights** offer reliable alternatives for getting between the larger towns. The key is to plan based on your comfort level with driving, the season, and how much of Iceland you want to see outside of the main tourist routes.

In the end, **renting a car** gives you the most control over your trip, but **public buses**, **domestic flights**, and **guided tours** all provide alternatives depending on your preferences and the time of year you visit.

10.2 PACKING

It's essential to really think about how the weather can change—fast. You could wake up to a bright, sunny day only to find yourself in the middle of wind, rain, or even snow later that afternoon. **That's Iceland for you**—unpredictable, stunning, and often chilly. So, when it comes to packing, it's all about balance and making sure you have exactly what you need to stay warm, dry, and comfortable, without overpacking. It's a game of layers, waterproof gear, and practical items, tailored to each season and the unique environment you're about to explore.

For Spring (March-May), you're looking at temperatures that hover between **0°C and 10°C (32°F to 50°F)**. It's a time of year when **winter still lingers**, so expect cold mornings, chilly evenings, and rain in between. You're going to want to layer up. **Start with thermals**, and I mean real thermals. **Merino wool is your best friend here**, not just because it keeps you warm, but also because it stays warm even when it's wet. You'll need that. Now, over your base layer, add something insulating—**a fleece jacket or wool sweater**, something you can pull off if the sun decides to break through. But don't skip the outer shell. **Waterproof and windproof jacket and pants are non-negotiable.** The wind, especially near the coast, can feel biting, and Icelandic rain doesn't play. You'll be surprised how suddenly it can come down.

Your footwear? **Waterproof hiking boots.** You'll be walking through muddy trails, wet rocks, and likely more than one puddle. If your feet get wet, your day is ruined, so make sure those boots are durable and comfortable for long walks. And of course, don't forget **a warm hat, gloves, and scarf**. You'll thank yourself when the wind whips through. And, because Iceland has geothermal pools every-where, pack a **swimsuit**, even in spring. Trust me, there's nothing like soaking in hot water while it's cold outside.

When it comes to **summer (June-August)**, it's not like most people's idea of summer. The temperatures sit around **10°C to 15°C (50°F to 60°F)**, so while it's warmer, you're still going to want to layer. **Light thermals for the morning**, especially if you're an early riser, are still a good idea. Mornings are cool, and by mid-afternoon, you might want to shed layers, but not too many. A **fleece or light sweater** will work for the middle of the day, but don't pack away your **waterproof jacket**—summer in Iceland doesn't mean it's dry. You'll still face sudden rains, especially if you're hanging out near waterfalls or along the coast.

Also, **sleep masks** become your best friend in the summer. **The midnight sun**, where it stays light almost all night, can throw off your sleep if you're not used to it, and blackout curtains aren't always a given. You might be able to sleep through anything, but a little mask can make all the difference in feeling refreshed for your next adventure.

Now, **autumn (September-November)** is a bit of a mixed bag. You'll find it feels a lot like **early winter**—temperatures range from **0°C to 10°C (32°F to 50°F)**. You'll want to gear up similarly to spring: **thermal layers** (again, I swear by merino wool), **insulating sweaters**, and **waterproof outer layers**. But here's where you start thinking about **crampons**. Yes, crampons—those spiked cleats you attach to your boots. You might encounter early snow or ice, especially on trails that see less foot traffic, and you'll want to keep your footing.

In the end, **winter (December-February)**. The cold is real, with temperatures between **-10°C and 5°C (14°F to 41°F)**. You're going to need the works. **Thick thermals**, not just for warmth but because Icelandic winds find their way through even the smallest gaps. **A heavy fleece or down layer** is absolutely necessary. And on top of that, you'll want a **waterproof and windproof winter coat**, something long enough to cover your legs from that cold breeze. **Insulated, water-proof boots** are non-negotiable. You'll be walking through snow and maybe ice, and if your feet get cold, the rest of your body follows quickly. Hats, gloves, and scarves are a given, but think about investing in **hand warmers** or other **heat packs** for those extra cold days, particularly if you're planning long outdoor excursions. **Crampons** are essential for safety—**you don't want to be slipping** on icy trails when you're supposed to be enjoying the view.

Regardless of when you go, a few essentials should always make it into your suitcase. **A universal power adapter**—you'll need it for your electronics, and Iceland uses **Type C and F plugs**, with **220V voltage**. A **reusable water bottle** is perfect because the tap water here is some of the cleanest in the world, so refill and stay hydrated without worrying about buying bottled water. And for those longer days out, especially if you're road-tripping, make sure to carry a **portable** charger—you don't want your phone dying just when you need your map or want to snap a photo of that epic landscape.

10.3 BUDGET TIPS

When you are on a budget, you'll need to take each aspect carefully, making sure that every penny is well spent because, as you might already know, Iceland can get expensive if you don't plan wisely. For the first let's see the **accommodation options**, where you can really stretch your budget a little bit. If you don't mind communal living and meeting new people, then **hostels** will likely be your best bet. In cities like Reykjavik or Akureyri, hostel prices range from **4,000 ISK to 7,000 ISK** per night, depending on the season and whether you're opting for a bed in a shared dorm or a more private option. The real benefit here is that many hostels come with **kitchen facilities**, allowing you to cook your own meals, which is a massive cost-saver. Just think about it, instead of spending **2,000 to 3,000 ISK** on a meal at a restaurant, you could pick up ingredients at a supermarket and prepare a meal for a fraction of that cost.

If you prefer a bit more privacy but still want to keep things afford-able, **guesthouses** are an excellent middle ground. Prices for guest-houses typically range from **8,000 ISK to 15,000 ISK** per night, and they're often cozy, with a more personal, local touch. You'll find guest-houses not just in Reykjavik but also in rural areas, where they can serve as perfect base camps for exploring nearby attractions. Some even include breakfast in the price, which can save you money on your first meal of the day.

Now, if you're visiting during the warmer months—typically from **May to September**—camping is an even more budget-friendly option and offers a unique way to experience Iceland's incredible landscapes. At around **1,500 ISK per night** for a spot in a campground, you can wake up to stunning views without breaking the bank. Campsites are found throughout Iceland, often close to major attractions, and many offer decent facilities like showers and kitchens. Not to mention, with Iceland's almost 24-hour daylight during the summer, camping gives you a flexible and adventurous way to explore at your own pace. Just make sure you're well-prepared for the unpredictable weather, even in the summer.

For the **food**, dining out every day can really eat into your budget. The average meal in a mid-range restaurant can cost anywhere from **2,500 ISK to 5,000 ISK**, which is why many budget-conscious travelers choose to visit supermarkets like **Bónus**, **Krónan**, or **Nettó**. These are your best options for picking up groceries at reasonable prices, allowing you to prepare your own meals. Staples like pasta, rice, bread, vegetables, and canned goods are affordable, and you can easily pack snacks for a day of exploring. Another good idea is to stop by local bakeries for cheaper meal options like **sandwiches** and **pastries**, where you can find something for **500 to 1,500 ISK**.

For those moments when you want to eat out but not splurge, look out for **food trucks** or budget-friendly restaurants. In Reykjavik, for example, you can grab a delicious **Icelandic hot dog** from the iconic **Bæjarins Beztu Pylsur** for around **500 ISK**. Another smart choice is hitting up some of the local **buffets**—they're not always super cheap, but you get a good variety of food, which can make the cost worthwhile if you're really hungry. I Suggest!

Transportation can be tricky, but with some planning, you can avoid overspending. If you're sticking to Reykjavik and the surrounding areas, **public buses** are your best bet. A single ride costs **470 ISK**, or you can buy a **day pass for 1,700 ISK** for unlimited rides. The public bus system also extends to rural areas with the **Straeto buses**, but long-distance travel can get pricey. For instance, a one-way ticket from Reykjavik to Akureyri costs around **7,000 to 9,000 ISK**. However, if you prefer a more flexible travel experience, **renting a car** might be the way to go. A small, fuel-efficient car typically costs around **6,000 to 10,000 ISK per day** depending on the season, but keep in mind that **fuel costs** are high, averaging about **250 ISK per liter**. Renting a car gives you the freedom to explore more remote areas that aren't as accessible by bus, and if you're traveling with a group, the cost can be shared, making it more affordable. **Hitchhiking** is also fairly common in Iceland and generally considered safe, especially in rural areas, where locals are known to be helpful.

Once you have your transportation sorted, you can save a lot of money by focusing on **free or low-cost attractions**. Many of Iceland's most stunning sites—**waterfalls, hiking trails, geothermal springs**— are free to visit. For example, visiting **Seljalandsfoss, Skógafoss**, or the **black sand beaches of Reynisfjara** costs you nothing but gas to get there. Reykjavik offers **free walking tours**, where knowledgeable guides take you through the city's highlights—you can tip them at the end based on how much you enjoyed the tour. To further stretch your budget, look out for **money-saving passes**, like the **Reykjavik City Card**, which gives you free access to several museums, galleries, and public swimming pools in the city, as well as unlimited public transport for **24 hours** at about **4,000 ISK**. The card also offers discounts at certain shops and restaurants.

In the end, as you may know already, always book as far in

advance as possible. Prices for flights, accommodations, and even some tours can skyrocket during high tourist season, which is typically between **June and August**. If you're planning to rent a car or join a specific tour, booking early will not only save you money but also ensure availability, especially for popular activities like **glacier hiking** or **whale watching**.

10.4 SAFETY AND EMERGENCY INFORMATION

Safety and awareness are two things you simply cannot overlook. **The weather here can change faster than you think**—and it often does. You'll start your day with blue skies and sunshine, only to find the clouds rolling in a few hours later, bringing rain, wind, or even snow, depending on the season. This isn't something you can afford to ignore, so make it a habit to stay informed. You'll want to check **vedur.is**, the site for the Meteorological Office, before heading out every morning. Don't just glance at it—pay attention to any warnings or sudden shifts. It's not uncommon to have road closures or dangerous wind conditions, especially in exposed areas like the south coast or the highlands. You might also want to download a reliable weather app like **Yr.no**, which gives detailed updates on conditions throughout the day. You won't be surprised by an unexpected storm if you make checking the weather part of your routine, and it's crucial because this unpredictability is part of what makes this place both beautiful and challenging.

If you're planning on driving, let's talk about **road conditions**. The main highways, like **Route 1**, are paved and easy to navigate, but the further you get from populated areas, the more likely you are to encounter **gravel roads**, which can be tricky. Driving on gravel requires more control—keep your speed in check, particularly on sharp turns or near cliffs. Then there are the **single-lane bridges**, a common sight once you're outside of Reykjavik. These narrow stretches require you to yield to oncoming traffic, and it's always a good idea to slow down and take turns with other drivers. If you're new to these roads, drive slowly until you get the hang of it.

Now, let's talk about the **F-roads**—these are highland roads, and they're an entirely different story. These are only open in summer, and they require a **4x4 vehicle**. They're not just gravel; they're rugged, full of obstacles like rivers you'll have to ford, and only accessible if you're experienced or going with a guide. Trust me, these aren't roads you can take lightly, and if you're unsure, it's better to skip them or book a tour that knows how to navigate them. It's not just about having the right car; it's about knowing how to handle the unpredictable terrain that comes with it.

Remember to always have your **headlights on**, even in the middle of the day—this is the law, no exceptions. You'll also notice the speed limits are lower than you might expect, with **90 km/h** being the maximum on highways, and even lower on gravel roads, around **80 km/h**. These limits are there for your safety because many roads can become dangerous due to weather or unexpected wildlife crossing. Speaking of which, **sheep on the road** are a common sight, especially in rural areas. They can dart out unexpectedly, and they don't always stick to the side of the road, so slow down when you see them.

In case of an emergency, dialing **112** will connect you with emergency services, whether you need police, fire services, or an ambulance. But if you're venturing into remote areas or hiking in the highlands, it's wise to file your travel plans with **Safetravel.is**. This free service allows the **Icelandic Search and Rescue** (ICE-SAR) to know your whereabouts in case something goes wrong. This step is often overlooked but could be life-saving.

When you visit the geothermal areas like **Geysir** or **Haukadalur**, **stay on marked paths** at all times. The ground may look solid, but just underneath lies boiling water that can seriously injure you. Follow posted warnings, and don't get too close to geysers, even when they're not active—it's unpredictable terrain, and accidents happen when people aren't careful.

If you're headed toward **volcanic regions**, pay attention to any signs or alerts about volcanic activity. **Eruptions** can happen, though they're usually well-monitored, and warnings are issued in advance. But it's still good to know what to do and where to go in case something happens.

If you want to vist **glaciers**, safety should always be your number one concern. These glaciers are incredibly dangerous if you're not properly prepared. You should never venture onto one without a **certified guide**. They'll have the proper equipment, like crampons and ropes, and they know how to handle the unpredictable ice formations, including dangerous **crevasses**. Every year, tourists are injured or worse because they didn't take the proper precautions. Play it smart, and always book a guided tour for glaciers.

The beach may sound like a peaceful place to relax, but beaches like **Reynisfjara** come with hidden dangers. The **sneaker waves** are infamous here, and they can catch you off guard, pulling you into the cold Atlantic waters in seconds. Even on a calm day, the waves are unpredictable. So, always stay well back from the waterline, no matter how tempting it is to get close for a better look at the basalt columns.

Should you need medical care, the healthcare system is excellent, but the **main hospitals** are in Reykjavik. Smaller towns will have **health clinics**, but their services may be limited. **Pharmacies**, called **Apótek**, are common and well-stocked, but it's a good idea to bring any prescription medications with you. If you're an EU citizen, carry your **EHIC card**—it gives you access to some medical services. However, no matter where you're from, having **travel insurance** that covers emergency medical situations and evacuation is essential, especially if you're doing any adventure activities.

One last thing—**mobile coverage** is generally good, but there are plenty of areas, especially in the highlands and some coastal regions, where you'll lose signal. It's best to have **offline maps** downloaded, and always inform someone of your travel plans if you're heading into remote regions.

I NEED A LOCAL SIM?

Once you land, one of the smartest things you can do is get yourself a local SIM card, and trust me, it's not just for convenience — it's practically a must, especially when you're going to be moving around a lot, exploring places beyond the main cities. Right when you arrive at **Keflavik International Airport**, you'll notice several shops or kiosks offering SIM cards tailored specifically for tourists. These are easy to spot and are priced reasonably — so it's ideal to grab one there. If you miss the chance at the airport, don't worry, you can easily pick one up in **Reykjavik** at almost any gas station or convenience store. Even supermarkets like **Krónan** or **Bonus** stock SIM cards.

Here's the key detail: the main providers you'll come across are **Síminn**, **Vodafone**, and **Nova**. These three cover pretty much the entire country, though if you're heading into more remote areas, **Síminn** tends to have the best coverage overall. Prices for SIM cards usually range between **ISK 2,900** and **ISK 5,000**, depending on how much data you think you'll need. Typically, you'll get anywhere from **5 to 10 GB of data**, which should be plenty for navigating, checking the weather, or even streaming if you're using it wisely. Most SIM cards also come with a small allowance for local calls and texts, just in case you need to make arrangements while on the go.

Before you buy, i suggest you to make sure your phone is **unlocked**, this is important. If it's locked to your home carrier, you won't be able to use the Icelandic SIM, and you could end up stuck with hefty roaming charges from your provider back home. No one wants that. If you've checked and your phone is ready, all you have to do is pop the SIM in, restart your phone, and you should be good to go. Sometimes you might need to enter a quick activation code that comes with the card, but it's straightforward.

Now, why should you bother with a local SIM? Aside from avoiding outrageous roaming fees, having local data is essential, especially when you're traveling outside of major towns. **Wi-Fi** is easy to find in most accommodations, cafes, and restaurants, but once you start exploring beyond the cities, you'll find yourself without a signal in many places. Popular tourist spots like hiking trails, remote beaches, or even parts of the **Golden Circle** may not have Wi-Fi, so mobile data is going to be your lifeline.

Think of all the tools you'll need (even if you may know already): **Google Maps** to navigate, apps like **Vedur.is** for real-time weather updates, or **Safetravel.is** to keep you informed about road conditions, safety alerts, or even emergency notifications. These services will only work if you have a stable connection. And if you're heading into more isolated areas, being able to reach out in case of an emergency is vital.

In terms of tourist preferences, most visitors choose to use local SIM cards simply for the ease and cost-effectiveness. Renting a mobile Wi-Fi device is another option, but it's often more expensive, and keeping it charged can be a hassle, especially if you're hiking or driving long distances. A prepaid SIM lets you keep your phone in your pocket, no extra devices needed, and you're always connected, whether you're navigating remote **F-roads** or trying to locate a gas station.

CONCLUSION

Here we go..

As I sit here, reflecting on my time in Iceland, I can't help but think back to the very first moment that this country truly took my breath away. I remember standing under the midnight sky, bundled up against the cold, staring upward as the **Northern Lights** began to ripple across the heavens. It wasn't just the colors—the greens, purples, and blues—but the absolute quiet that came with it. Everything just… stopped. In that moment, it felt like the world had shifted, and all that existed was the sky and me. That's what Iceland does to you—it grabs you, shows you its magic, and leaves a mark that stays long after you've gone home.

But Iceland is more than its well-known natural wonders like the **Northern Lights** or the geysers. It's the little moments, the unexpected turns that turn a great trip into something unforgettable. One of my favorite memories was actually quite simple: driving along the **Ring Road**, pulling off to a random dirt path, and discovering a hidden waterfall that wasn't even on the map. No crowds, no signs, just the sound of rushing water and the solitude of nature. It's these surprises, these quiet corners of the country that make traveling here feel so personal.

When you visit, you'll experience that same feeling. Sure, you'll hit the main highlights—the powerful **Gullfoss**, the stunning **Reykjavik** streets full of color and culture, but it's those detours, those small unplanned moments that will linger with you the most. You'll find yourself thinking about the tiny, unmarked paths that lead to secret hot springs or quiet beaches where it's just you and the landscape. That's where the true magic of this place lies.

Iceland is a place where the land and the people are deeply connected. This isn't just some vacation spot where you come to snap a few photos and leave. The locals here have a deep respect for their environment, and once you're here, you'll understand why. It's not just about folklore (though the stories of the **Huldufólk** will charm you), it's about the understanding that this place is special, and it's up to all of us to preserve that. If you're hiking through the lava fields, resist the urge to build those little stone cairns for fun—leave the land as you found it. And when you're wandering through the moss-covered landscapes, remember it took centuries for that moss to grow—tread lightly.

Now, let's talk practical advice. If I learned anything on my trips to Iceland, it's that **layers are your best friend**. The weather here can change in an instant. One minute you're basking in sunshine, the next, you're pulling on a raincoat because a quick shower rolled in. And don't let that deter you. The unpredictability is part of the adventure. You'll laugh about that time you got caught in a sudden downpour while standing on a black sand beach or the moment you realized you needed sunglasses and a wool hat on the same day. Be prepared for it all—layers, waterproof gear, sturdy boots. Trust me, you'll be glad you packed for every season.

And here's something I didn't expect: **Iceland is incredibly safe and easy to navigate**. People are friendly, English is widely spoken, and the roads—though occasionally a bit wild—are well maintained. Renting a car is a fantastic way to see the island, and I highly recommend taking the time to drive the **Ring Road** if you can. Sure, it's not the fastest way to see everything, but it gives you the freedom to stop wherever your curiosity takes you.

And if you're wondering about timing, **each season offers something different**. I personally love visiting in late spring or early autumn when the crowds thin out but the landscapes are still full of life. Summer brings the **Midnight Sun**, and you'll have endless daylight to explore. Winter? That's Northern Lights season, and the country takes on a whole different beauty when blanketed in snow. Whenever you choose to visit, Iceland will show you something unique.

Before I wrap up, I just want to take a moment to say **thank you for trusting this guide on your journey**. It's been a labor of love to put this together, and if it's helped make your trip easier or more meaningful, that's all I could ask for. If you found this guide useful, I'd truly appreciate it if you left a review. It helps other travelers find the information they need, and it helps me improve future editions to ensure they're the best they can be. Your feedback is invaluable, and I'm grateful for your support.

Lastly, who knows? Maybe one day our paths will cross in this stunning land. Iceland has a way of pulling you back, time and time again, and perhaps we'll meet while wandering through one of those hidden trails or standing in awe of the Northern Lights. Safe travels, my friend—**may your Icelandic adventure be filled with moments that take your breath away**.

Made in the USA
Las Vegas, NV
14 November 2024

11806018R00073